LIFE'S
NON
CONFORMITIES

**An Auditor's Tale of Practical
Application of Social, Emotional
& Behavioral Strategies.**

By: Salman Raza

Copyright Notice

The names and identifying characteristics of some of the individuals featured throughout this book have been changed to protect their privacy.

TABLE OF CONTENTS

Acknowledgements

This project was not an individual effort. There were many people who were truly inspirational, and without their unconditional support, this book would have remained only a dream.

Since the book reflects my life experiences, acknowledgement must start from the beginning. I am immensely grateful to my parents and siblings for providing an ideal nurturing environment for me to grow. They instilled in me moral values, gave me the confidence to explore every aspect of life, and have always encouraged me to be inquisitive. It is these things that have progressively shaped my personality. Words can never be adequate to express the genuine sense of gratitude towards them, and I am extremely blessed to have them as my parents and siblings.

Even though my parents and siblings nurtured me in my childhood, and helped me grow my wings, my wife, Kiran, has been truly amazing. She along with our children Zain & Mishal continuously enable me to fly and realize my potential and dreams. People will only see my apparent work, but no one saw unconditional love, continuous encouragement, relentless support and immeasurable sacrifices of my beloved wife. She deserves accolades for this work more than I do. I cannot thank Kiran enough for putting up with my silly ambitions. She is my unsung hero and the best partner in crime anyone could ever imagine. I'm truly blessed to have her in my life.

Special thanks to Mr. Yasin Rahim, whose insistence literally dragged me out of my ignorance, introduced the concept of self-awareness, and opened my eyes to a new, peaceful and aware life that served as an inspiration for this book.

I cannot forget the contributions of Ms. Maria Pattinson, Mr. Aamer Naeem, Mr. Sarfaraz Jeeraj, Dr. Akber and my LDP friends for stimulating my desire to embark on this journey of self-awareness. They have been my vision community for many years and have always selflessly supported my enthusiasm for this work.

Finally, a heartfelt thank you to my publishing partner, Ms. Mary Anna Rodabaugh for her impeccable editing skills and for her help in preparing this manuscript. Her continued guidance undoubtedly helped me sail through the unchartered waters of book writing.

About the Author

Salman Raza is an auditor, presenter, father, husband, and life learner. With over ten years of experience in the auditing world, Salman has seen his share of fascinating events, met interesting, sometimes difficult people, and found himself in unwanted and unforeseen conflicts. Inspired by his never-ending curiosity, Salman has thrown himself into the deep end of learning about personality types, cultural influences, personal fulfillment, human interaction, and purpose.

Throughout this book, Salman shares his story—well, many stories—and theories that illuminate behaviors and ways of thinking in the simplest sense.

Introduction

I know that I know nothing. This is called the Socrates paradox. We as humans are unaware of many things. Simply put, we do not know what we do not know. Sounds simple, right? If you look at an iceberg, you only see the tip. If you know nothing about icebergs, you may think what you see is all that exists.

However, as many of us know, there is much more to icebergs than what meets the eye. We can say the same for people. There is much more to people than what we initially see. These missed or overlooked elements are exceptional examples of life's nonconformities.

When looking at the self, life's nonconformities happen when we don't fulfill our own expectations. We all have expectations. When what we expect is misaligned, we create a nonconformance. Sometimes it is small; other times it is greater.

There are so many lenses we can use to see the world. Many times, we limit ourselves to the few lenses we are most familiar with. This is called bias. When I was growing up, I remember learning about the enormous impact a drought was having on Ethiopia.

People were dying from hunger. They were skin over skeletons. The GDP growth rate was negative 11.1%. Having no other knowledge or exposure to Ethiopian life, that is all I knew. Naturally, I thought all Ethiopian people were malnourished and lived in poverty.

I was not exposed to anything related to Ethiopia until 2016. That is when I met and had the pleasure of spending time with a family from Ethiopia. They were educated, healthy, and very hospitable. My interest in business growth and emerging markets taught me that Ethiopia, nowadays, is one of the fastest growing economies, with an annual GDP growth rate of 10.2%.[1]

This resilient nation has turned their misfortunes around, and now Ethiopia has been a very prosperous country for many years. How wrong I was! I felt foolish for generalizing that all Ethiopians were malnourished and lived in poverty. I was unaware and lacked exposure that could have helped me reframe my flawed perceptions.

I have experienced numerous occasions where people view me as a tip of an iceberg. For example, when I moved from the UK to America, my family lived in a hotel until we could settle into a house. The housekeeping staff at the hotel were primarily Hispanic/Latino. One day I was walking down the hall, and one housekeeper started speaking to me in Spanish. I gave her quite the confused look.

"It's okay. You can speak Spanish here," she reassured me in English.

"But I don't speak Spanish," I told her with a smile.

Based on my complexion alone, she and many of her colleagues thought my family was Hispanic/Latino. I looked like them. That physical comparison was enough to draw an incorrect conclusion. When I think about that, I laugh. I'm sure it surprised her to hear my British accent.

These two examples prove to me perceptions and outdated information often mislead us. We use these perceptions to draw incorrect or wrong conclusions.

[1] "World Bank national accounts data, and OECD National Accounts data files [1982-2017]," The World Bank, accessed June 4, 2019, https://data.worldbank.org/indicator/NY.GDP.MKTP.KD.ZG?locations=ET.

Humans are creatures of comfort. We like to stay locked in our comfort zones. This is done rarely out of ignorance and more so out of routine and familiarity.

Throughout this book, I will share concepts, theories, and experiences that will help you flip a switch in your mind and in your heart. I will touch on how to motivate people to work effectively with you. We'll learn about conflict resolution, casual and likeable dealing, negotiation skills, how to defeat a passive-aggressor, and all-around people management. I will also discuss how you can handle conflicting interactions.

Then we'll look at the tools you can use to make these things possible. I will discuss the many ways you can grow in your self-awareness and awareness of others to foster peaceful connections with everyone you encounter, including maintaining a "mindful" presence and establishing heart-to-heart connections. This book does not offer a quick fix. There is no button that can make our weaknesses go away with one push. This book is one step on a lengthy journey ahead.

Despite this, I hope this book ignites a spark within you. I hope you ask questions. I hope it inspires you to learn more about these topics and the very things that ignite your curiosity. Life learners live the richest lives. By the time you have read and digested this wisdom, you will learn many things. You will learn that no two people are the same and that their minds perceive, receive, manifest, manipulate, process, and execute the same information differently.

Before we get started, I have an interesting story for you:

It was Monday morning, around 8:00 a.m., when 23-year-old Ellen got up, ate a quick breakfast, and walked to her yoga class. It was three blocks from her apartment. After an hour of stretching and meditation, she felt at peace with herself and the world around her. That is, until she got home. Upon reaching her front door, Ellen noticed it was ajar. At first, she thought she forgot to lock and close it, but then she remembered double-checking the knob to be sure she locked it before leaving. It was a habit instilled in her by her mother. Ellen's heart started beating rapidly, her face grew hot, and she felt dizzy. Someone had broken into her home.

Too scared to go inside to investigate, she immediately called her best friend Samantha and her neighbor, Randall, who lived three doors down. Ellen was hysterical and almost hyperventilating when the pair arrived. Samantha tried to calm her, assuring her that everything would eventually be okay. Ellen wanted to go inside to assess the damage, but Randall told her not to until they called the police. He offered his apartment as a gathering place.

"We need to call the police and then a locksmith to change the locks and secure the apartment," Randall told Ellen and Samantha.

Ellen continued to sob uncontrollably.

"We need to just take a beat, Randall. Ellen just went through something terrifying. Let's just calm down and get our head straight before we do anything."

"She needs to ask the neighbors if they saw anything," Randall replied. "She needs to do an assessment of what is missing after that."

"She needs to process what just happened," Samantha chided, shooting Randall an icy look.

"I'm calling the cops," Randall said. "She needs to file a police report right now."

"Randall, just wait a few minutes. We're safe in your apartment for now. Give it a moment."

Samantha could not understand why Randall was not trying to comfort his neighbor. Ellen and Randall were friends, going out for lunch from time to time. He wasn't able to acknowledge that his friend was so upset she could not deal with the situation until she calmed down.

"What if the robber comes back? What if someone threatens me if I call the cops?" Ellen asked in between gasping sobs.

"Let's just take a deep breath and not worry about that right now," Samantha told her while patting Ellen's back gently.

"No, we should worry about it. She is right. They could come back. They usually don't, but you never know," Randall said. "Do you own a gun, Ellen?"

"Why would you ask her that?"

"She might need one for protection."

Without warning, Ellen stood up from the couch and stormed out of Randall's apartment. Her friends quickly followed suit.

"Don't go in yet, the police need to process the crime scene," Randall said. "There could be fingerprints or evidence in there."

Ellen walked to the side of her apartment and peered in the window.

"Oh, my God!" Ellen gasped. "My stuff is everywhere. My dining room table is on its side. There's broken glass everywhere! They have ransacked the place! They went through everything!"

"Let's go back to Randall's apartment," Samantha urged.

"Let's call the police right now. Enough procrastinating," Randall retorted.

Samantha was addressing Ellen's emotional situation. She was validating her friend's feelings of fear and uncertainty. Randall was assessing her literal problem and evaluating her physical safety and security. Both friends were doing what they thought was the right thing. Both lines of thinking were valid and appropriate, but who was right? If you found yourself in this situation, would you be Samantha or Randall?

There are certain personality traits that influence how we behave in any situation. Some of us are drawn towards feelings and emotions first, and others gravitate toward logic and reason. The key is to establish an awareness of not only the personality traits that make you tick, but also those around you.

When presented with this story for the first time, I eagerly awaited the answer. As an analytical person, I wanted to know what the right answer was. The fact is the answer is both lines of thinking are correct. The two friends addressed Ellen's situation in two very different ways, but neither was wrong.

As you journey through this book, the stories shared are a reflection of what I felt and what I recall. It contains my perspective of how events and situations unfolded. I believe everyone within these stories has been put in my life for a reason. To honor that, I have changed names to protect the privacy of these individuals. Thank you and enjoy the journey.

Salman Raza

Chapter 1: Fear in the Auditing Field

Have you ever feared for your life? I have, occasionally, but one such experience comes to the forefront of my mind.

I am an auditor. I work for a certification/accreditation service provider. We assess ISO (International Organization for Standardization) standards and regulatory requirements for the medical device industry. I go to medical device manufacturing companies, and I audit the business management systems. I assess how good their processes are and how effective their product design is. I review processes and documentation for their policies, objectives, design, manufacturing, purchasing, training, and problem-solving processes. I also review how the company meets the assessment criteria. These certifications enable manufacturers to license, register, and consequently sell their products in highly regulated health care facilities globally.

At least 250 days out of the year, I'm meeting new people, learning what they are doing and how they are doing it. Then I make an assessment on how well they are following the laws and rules of medical device regulations.

By the very nature of this exercise of "auditing," it involves a lot of questions. These questions often challenge the current practice. Because of these interactions, I get to experience a full spectrum of emotions. Basically, I'm meeting anywhere from four hundred to one thousand new people—with their many emotions and expectations—every year. That is a lot of first impressions.

My first encounter with my client Colton Barns was one I will never forget. It started with a customary phone call.

"You wanna get an earlier flight in, and I will pick you up from the airport?" Colton Barns asked.

"That is not necessary," I replied. "I am getting in late, but I will rent a car and drive to you."

"Naw, I got you. Call me when you land," Colton argued in a distinct Southern drawl.

It was election day 2016, and I had just wrapped up with a client in Arab, Alabama. In a week I would travel to Colton's company in Tuscaloosa, Alabama. As a courtesy, I called him to work out the details of my upcoming assessment. I was planning on traveling late in the evening from my home in Houston, so I could have dinner with my family before my departure.

"Can't you stay, Daddy?" my six-year-old daughter asked me before I left for Arab.

I wanted to put my two children to bed and read them a bedtime story before leaving for my work trip. I travel a lot for my job, and I really cherish those stolen moments I get to have with my family. I understood that Colton was trying to mitigate the cost of this trip. If he picked me up and drove me, his company would not be responsible for the rental car charge.

I pulled the phone from my ear and sighed. If Colton did not want to pay for the rental car, he could easily discuss it with my company's customer care department. If deemed appropriate, they would find a way to address his concern. From my perspective, there was no need for an escort to this audit.

"Take an earlier flight, and I will pick ya up," he urged.

"Thank you, but I'm going to keep the flight and schedule I already have."

Finally, he let the details of my travel rest.

"Say, where you from? You have an accent," he abruptly asked me, changing the subject.

It was a question I was used to.

"I'm from the UK."

"Really? Does not sound like an English name!"

I thought this was a little abrupt, but it's true. I don't have an "English" name. I sighed in agreement.

"You guys just had the Brexit. Things will really change around your land. They're kicking immigrants out. Policies are favoring those who were there first. I bet Spain and Germany will see big changes too," he said proudly.

He had no idea what he was talking about.

When the UK voted to leave the European Union (EU), an economic and political partnership involving 28 European countries, the decision was based on much more than immigration.

The term "immigration" means something quite different in the UK compared to how immigration is perceived in America. Americans see a lot of negative stories on cable news about immigrants from other countries. In January 2017, President Trump issued a travel ban on immigrants coming out of certain Muslim countries to the US.

From talks about building a wall to stricter immigration laws, the overall connotation disseminated throughout America is that "immigration is bad." When Americans get most of their information about international affairs from cable news, the channel of information can be narrow and biased.

In the UK, before Brexit, immigration was less about "foreign" people trying to enter the land and more about those in the EU moving about other EU countries. This was true for relatively newly accessed EU member states such as Poland, Bulgaria, and Croatia. Even then, for most of the population, immigration was not an issue. Traditionalists and purists never liked taking instructions from EU parliament.

Frail economies in some member states (Greece and Portugal, to name a few) meant other member states had to bail them out to keep the Union economically sustainable. As someone who lived in the UK, I knew much more about the topic than Colton.

Instead of taking this moment of ignorance and turning it into a teachable moment, I shifted the focus back to my upcoming visit. We worked out the details of the audit, and I told him I would see him in a week. I knew this audit would be interesting, but I did not understand just how memorable it would be.

I had been doing this kind of work for over a decade. Before I became a European notified body/registrar auditor, I worked for a medical device company as a research-and-development and compliance engineer. I had the experience of entertaining auditors from external bodies and regulators. Being on both sides of the auditing relationship has given me a great deal of perspective. I know what it is like to have someone come into my place of work and request all types of documents. It feels like you're being evaluated under a microscope. When my company was being audited, there were several occasions where we were deemed noncompliant in certain areas. I now use these stories with my clients, so they understand that I know what they are going through.

Colton Barns would be different.

As my plane landed at Tuscaloosa Regional Airport, I smiled to myself remembering my evening with my family. True to my plan, I enjoyed a delightful meal with my wife and children before tucking my son and daughter into bed for the night. I read them one of their favorite stories and watched them fall asleep before leaving for this trip. Those moments are precious to me.

One week prior, Mr. Donald Trump was elected President of the US. The country was more polarized than ever. Everyone had very strong feelings and opinions on either side of the political spectrum. Much like political districts, the feelings and viewpoints varied by geographic location. People were hungry for change.

Frequently, my work sends me to large cities where you can't walk around the block without encountering an immigrant. I was born in Pakistan, went to graduate school in Australia, and lived in the UK for many years before moving to the US. I look like and sound like an immigrant. President Trump feels strongly about immigrants. People who fully support President Trump might also feel strongly about immigrants. The news prominently featured hate crimes against immigrants.

Over half of Alabama voted for Trump. (Although that did not mean I had anything to fear, I too was feeling a little apprehensive because of what they featured in the news.) I spent Election Day in Arab, Alabama, and encountered some of the nicest and most hospitable people you would ever meet. Many of them supported President Trump. Everyone was polite and professional. I knew not to stereotype people based on where they live, but in the back of my mind I knew I had to be prepared. I got to my hotel well after midnight and went straight to bed to prepare for my early start.

It was a refreshing morning, not too cold and not too warm. The drive was a blur of picturesque farmland. In a little over twenty minutes, I arrived at my destination. I pulled off the main road into a commercial plaza. Colton's business was nestled in a rundown shopping center between a janitorial supply store and a gun and ammo shop. The premises looked small from the outside. Sometimes the companies I audit host all their production and manufacturing of devices on site. Other companies, like Colton's, purchase medical device equipment from other vendors to sell to their customers.

As I walked inside, an unfamiliar and slightly unpleasant smell greeted me. There were two rooms that looked like offices and a restroom off to the side. The beige carpet had several noticeable yet unidentifiable stains on it.

"Hello there, how can I help you?" a middle-aged woman with curly brown hair asked. She was sitting at a desk off in the corner. I assumed she was Colton's secretary.

Before I could answer, Colton came out of his office and walked to the center of the room. He was an older man, maybe in his mid- to late 60s, stocky, clean shaven, with white hair. He was very tall, about 6'3", and he wasn't wearing shoes. He walked toward me and shook my hand—a firm but sweaty handshake.

"Welcome." He gave me an unfamiliar gaze. "Don't really see your kind in this job!"

I didn't really know how to respond to this, so I just introduced myself and glanced down at his bright-red socks.

"Yeah, my feet swell up from time to time, and I got to air them out for a bit. Makes it painful to walk in shoes," he said nonchalantly.

I smiled and nodded. "May I use the restroom before we begin?" I asked.

"Help yourself."

I walked inside and immediately regretted it. The toilet bowl had brown stains along the rim. The sink looked like it hadn't been cleaned in years. A half-empty bottle of coagulated soap sat on top of the toilet. It smelled like raw sewage. I couldn't stand it, so I held it and quickly exited the disgusting facilities.

Colton invited me into his office. I should not have been surprised by my surroundings, but once again I found myself at a loss for words. Colton had a small office, overtaken by an enormous desk and oversized maroon chair. There was a small table next to his desk. Every single surface was covered with papers, folders, trash, you name it.

As I walked into the room, I was trying to be careful not to step on anything on the floor, which was proving to be an impossible task. As I made my way to an open chair, I noticed a rifle leaning against the corner of the wall behind Colton's desk. I looked away quickly, knowing a lingering stare could somehow prompt a conversation about firearms.

I have lived in three different countries prior to my move to the US. It was never legal in my former countries to own a firearm, let alone have it lying around unlocked and in the open. I had never seen one casually hanging out in an office before.

Colton slouched back in his chair with a nonchalance that

made me realize he wasn't taking the audit seriously. Perhaps he wasn't taking me seriously. I was beginning to wonder if the firearm was positioned in my line of sight to intimidate me.

"All right let's get started," I said with a smile.

As we were going through the documents, I learned that Colton used to have a clean room nearby. A clean room is a controlled area for working with sensitive material that cannot be exposed to contaminants.

Medical device companies that produce items that are implanted in the body need to be sterilized for safety. Sterilization takes place in clean rooms.

All the entrants of these clean rooms must observe strict gowning protocols. Colton's clean room was shut down by the Food and Drug Administration after a federal regulator inspected the property and determined it did not meet the specifically required standards and regulations. for ISO 14644-1 Class 3: Clean Rooms.

"The clean room got shut down because of Obama," Colton said. "It is his fault. The FDA inspector said they were here on executive orders from the president, and that is why they had to shut me down."

He was dead serious. As we addressed concerns throughout my audit, Colton somehow steered the conversation to what I learned was his favorite topic: blaming Obama for everything that went wrong with his business and the entire world. He just could not comprehend any other reason for noncompliance. I started to get nervous.

Colton was clearly a very opinionated man with strong, if not stubborn, beliefs. I was an auditor doing my job, but there would be plenty of issues I had to bring up that he probably would not like. He could not blame all of them on Obama. Obama did not write the policies and procedures Colton was out of compliance with. He would eventually have to take responsibility for his own actions. What did that mean for me?

Colton took every opportunity to remind me how things were "finally going to change" now that we would have the right man for the job in the Oval Office. "Isn't it great?" he would ask me. "Trump will change things and move this country in the right direction. I'm thrilled. It is about damn time." He would slam his fist happily against the desk, startling me. I tried not to jump.

He would look at me, seeking my argument or agreement. A sly smile spread across his face as he looked through me with challenging eyes. I gave him neither. I responded with things such as "I'm glad you're happy, that is great for you" in the least passive-aggressive way possible.

I knew little about American politics, but I knew medical device regulations and FDA's modus operandi, so I stuck to that. Last I checked, the FDA does not shut down clean rooms because the president orders them to do so. The only way it is possible is when the FDA has objective evidence that the clean room is contaminated.

I also had to be conscientious about my facial expressions. I had to look and act the part, all while staying true to myself. It was difficult. Not to mention the fact Colton kept praising President Trump's stance on immigration in front of an immigrant. I could not tell if he was trying to provoke me or was just ignorant to the fact that I was nonwhite and an immigrant. I suspected he might look for an excuse to pull that firearm on me. I got a sense it was a mix of motivations.

Colton mentioned several times that soon-to-be US attorney general and former Alabama senator Jeff Sessions was a close friend of his. He felt proud of this connection. I suppose I would feel proud, too, if I were in his shoes. There is nothing wrong with proclaiming that connection, but as a brown immigrant I felt his mention had a deliberate undertone. My palms started to sweat as a feeling of discomfort washed over me.

While Colton looked at his computer, I glanced over at the gun again. My heart raced. I felt trapped. Here I was with this man, with an obvious aversion to my race, enclosed in a tiny office with a weapon in the corner. I would have to tell him many things he would not like. He would eventually run out of excuses and people to blame. He would be a hard person to say "no" to. I worried that just by doing my job, I would soon create a hostile environment.

The uncomfortable exchange went on for about a half hour before Colton said he had to finish up a quick job and asked me to leave his office. I had a feeling he did not consider me important enough to take up his time, so he palmed me off to Betty, his secretary.

Had we just started the audit meeting, or had Colton just spent the last half hour trying to "put me in my place"?

"You can go on over to Betty for the rest. She'll get you what you need. I have to take care of something quick," he said.

I gathered my things and walked back out into the front office area.

"All right, so what do you need?" Betty asked me. She smiled. Betty had kind eyes but a vacant expression -- like she was trying to figure out what day it was or why she was working. I picked up where Colton and I left off. "This document is outdated. Do you have a recent copy available? You should update it every few years."

She took the paper from my hand and looked at it for a long time, as if she were trying to translate a foreign language.

"Colton? Do we have an update of this document?" Betty yelled across the room to her boss's open office door. I held my breath. My heart skipped a beat and not in a good way. It worried me that Colton would be angry.

Colton stepped out and walked over, taking the document from Betty's hand. He glanced at me. I couldn't tell if he was angry or not. He raised his eyebrows and said, "Let me look in my office." I exhaled slowly.

Colton returned to his office, and I moved on to the next thing. I kept finding issues. Documents were outdated. Critical information was missing. They created some documents for the company with language for a large corporation, not an outfit of two employees. There were procedures for manufacturing, but this company did not manufacture any product on-site. From an auditing perspective, it was a mess.

Every time I asked Betty a question, she would look at me with a very confused expression. After holding that gaze for a few moments, she'd ultimately yell the question back to Colton, who would sometimes answer from his office and other times step out to explain things. It was one of the most bizarre audits I had ever conducted.

Every time Colton emerged from his office; I was nervous he would be angry. He had pawned me off on Betty to work on this evaluation but was interrupted every couple of minutes. He was getting impatient but continued to comply.

On several occasions, I referred to my audit and soft-skills training. I considered my next move. Instead of using my opinion, I would not compare Colton's documents with industry-best practice or other companies. I would not let his opinion of me or "my kind" cloud my judgment. I would remain objective and ask myself, "Is it compliant or not?" Colton's documents did not need to be the best. They just had to be compliant or not. Whether or not I liked the documents was irrelevant.

Unfortunately, I was finding many things that were not compliant. I would have to tell Colton that his company had numerous major nonconformities and that my company (as the notified body and registrar) could not approve his products until he made significant changes. I dreaded that conversation.

Mercifully, lunch time arrived. Colton suggested the two of us go to a local Panera for a bite to eat. Ever wanting control of the situation, he insisted on driving. He knew the area better than me, so I obliged.

Colton led me to his beat-up car. It was an old Mazda and smelled worse than his office. Just like the carpet, the seats had unrecognizable stains. He did not put on his seatbelt. When he pulled out of the parking lot, I noticed the seat-belt indicator wasn't beeping. I wondered if old cars even had those indicators or if maybe he had it disconnected.

He talked about college football, praising the local team. I don't follow college football, so I just let him talk, adding acknowledgments that I was listening at appropriate times.

When we arrived at Panera, I immediately excused myself to go use the restroom. I had been holding it for four hours! It felt like it was the most beautiful bathroom I had ever seen -- clean with fresh soap and no stains or smells. I was relieved, literally.

Feeling much better, I ordered lunch, and we sat down at a booth toward the back. I still didn't know what to think about Colton, and I don't think he knew what to make of me either. I sat with my back to the restaurant, making sure I was not pinned in the booth should a disagreement arise.

He appeared to be a strong-willed man, set in his values. I wasn't sure what we'd talk about over lunch. I did not want to get into politics again, nor did I want to talk about myself. I wanted to know a little more about him, maybe get a read on him. Unfortunately, he took control of the conversation immediately.

"You say you're British?" Colton asked me abruptly. "You have the accent, but you don't look British. Where you from?"

It was the question that nearly every nonwhite person gets. "Where are you from?" Even people of different nationalities born in the US get asked that question. I always find it funny when you hear about someone like Colton asking someone of Southeastern Asian descent where they are from and they answer, "Brooklyn or Austin," or some US city, knowing that is not the answer the person is looking for.

"My parents are from Pakistan," I replied cautiously.

I felt uneasy again. After spending the morning with Colton, I had a good idea how he felt about people of different complexions, people from countries like Pakistan, and immigrants. Colton clenched his jaw ever so slightly.

"I see," Colton said.

I hate to admit it, but a feeling of embarrassment overcame me. I later came to realize that this was the demon I was battling with that day. I am of Pakistani origin. I am proud of my heritage and my country, but I felt apprehensive about telling Colton. I felt his perception of my origin would give him further cause to undermine me.

I quickly reminded myself that I'm proud of my heritage. I took inspiration from one of my favorite quotes from *Game of Thrones*, season one, episode one. When Tyrion Lannister notices Jon Snow's feelings about the fact he was the bastard son of Ned Stark, he offers his advice.

He says, "Let me give you some counsel, bastard. Never forget what you are, for surely the world will not. Make it your strength. Then it can never be your weakness. Armor yourself in it, and it will never be used to hurt you."[2] Well said, Tyrion.

I took a bite of my sandwich and avoided eye contact. Desperate to change the subject, I asked him if he always worked for himself or if this was the first time.

"I used to work as a sales representative years ago," he replied. "How much do you travel for work?"

I told him that my job is 95% travel, and I am sent to places all over the country. I told him it was an enjoyable job, but there were many times I missed being home with my wife and children. I did not want to get too personal with him. I was hoping to switch the conversation back to him and his life so we could stop talking about mine.

"Yeah, I used to travel a lot. I almost got divorced because of it," Colton said. It was the first personal and nonpolitical thing he shared with me. Notably, somehow, his divorce was not Obama's fault.

"Clearly you have worked your entire life," I said. "Why are

---

2 *Martin George R. R., A Game of Thrones (Bantam Spectra, 1996); 54*

you still working? Wouldn't you rather be enjoying retirement and playing golf?"

He looked down at his hands and looked back at me. "Honestly, I owe this company to someone. I promised my granddaughter that I would take care of her. So, I am doing everything I can to make this company stable and profitable. I want to give it to her once it's back up and running with regulatory approvals for the US and EU."

"Oh, okay," I replied. I wasn't sure if I could venture deeper into this topic, or if I had to let it rest. I stayed quiet to see if Colton would continue. He finished his sandwich in silence.

At the time, I did not know now that this tiny piece of information would be the one thing that got me through the audit — a breakthrough of sorts. It would be the emotional ammunition I needed against Colton's lethal ammunition. We finished our lunch and got back in the nasty old car. I spent the afternoon getting as much work done as I could, despite the excuses and explanations they offered, every time I had a question.

I wrapped up around 5:00 p.m. and went to my hotel. I was dreading the next day. Based on the stages of the audit we completed, Colton's company had numerous deficiencies, including at least three major areas of concern. Without a doubt, he would receive multiple nonconformities.

I would not recommend my company's certification for his management system or the CE mark for the products he was trying to sell in Europe. I did not think he trusted me, and I knew his political views could work against me. What if I made him so upset that he pulled a gun on me? What if he did not agree with my assessment and called the police to start some trouble? As I lay in bed, a few scenarios played out in my head. All of them were tragic.

Maybe I could just leave. Maybe I could book a flight out of there and go home. I had a job to do, but with each interaction, all I could envisage was Colton pulling that firearm on me. However, in my job, I never give up. Fight or flight? I wasn't sure what I would do.

After a sleepless night, I got up and prepared my things for the second day of the audit. I arrived around 8:15 a.m. Betty greeted me with an awkward smile as I walked in the door. I wasn't inside more than a few seconds before Colton popped out of his office. He was wearing shoes today.

"How'd you sleep?" he asked me.

I did not want to lie but did not want to tell him I had a rough night of sleep because I was worrying about his reaction to my report.

"Oh, as well as can be expected." That answer felt safe.

Colton walked over to Betty. As I walked toward his office, I noticed his product sitting on the shelf. It had a certification sticker from my company. It was a preemptive and illegal seal of approval. It was similar to a dental surgeon forging his dental school certificate and practicing illegally. I had to tell him. As if I did not have enough unfavorable news to share with him.

"Colton, your product has my company's certification sticker on it. We cannot place this on your products until the audit is complete and you've received formal certification from us. This is illegal," I said nervously.

"Ah, don't worry about that. We'll just take the stickers off for now," he replied nonchalantly.

I half expected him to shout at me for saying it was illegal, but he seemed to just shrug it off. It was a much bigger deal than what Colton was making of it. I made a notation so I would not forget to follow up.

We quickly got to work, finishing up the second half of the audit. Colton seemed to be in a pleasant mood, but I continued to find discrepancies. There were so many things wrong with this company. The list of things that needed to be corrected, continued to grow.

As the day went on, Colton became agitated. I think he had a sense for what my determination would be. Finally, it was time to have that hard conversation.

There have been many times in my career where I must explain the nonconforming issues to the client. No one is ever happy to hear these things, but I usually turn the conversation into a series of teachable moments. With Colton, I wasn't sure that would work. He seemed like a man who thought he knew everything.

This was the moment I had been dreading the entire time. I stalled. I looked at the front door, contemplating making a break for it. Perhaps I could say I left something at my hotel, and drive to the airport and fly to safety.

"All right, lay it on me."

I took a deep breath. Over the past two days, I felt violated because of several of his. Each one piled up in my mind. I should have been close to a breaking point, but after running the conversation over and over in my mind, I discovered a way I could address the verdict. I would deliver the message, do justice to my work, and discourage impulsive or violent reactions from the recipient.

"Let's forget about all of this audit stuff for a second," I said. "I really admire your desire and resolve to build this company. You're one determined and ambitious guy. You are noble in your intentions. I mean, you're preparing this company for your granddaughter. Who really does that type of gesture today? You are admirable and remarkable."

Colton raised his eyebrows. I continued.

"Based on the past two days, you know there are some things you will have to do. Let's make this company the ultimate gift, so your granddaughter believes you have changed her life with it."

Colton's face lit up. I could see his eyes start to water.

"That is all I want."

I explained the major nonconformities but was careful to do so in a manner where each nonconformance sounded like an opportunity for improvement instead of "something is wrong."

"Everything will be fine once you take care of these things. I know it does not sound pleasant right now. It is unfortunate," I said. "Perhaps it is a blessing in disguise. There are a few major areas of concern. I will submit my report to the technical department. I have only summarized my assessment commentary. They will overrule my commentary if I have made mistakes. Someone from my company will get back to you."

My heart was still racing. I could feel the sweat from my palms. I looked at Colton, waiting for an argument or an outburst or for him to blame Obama again. Instead, he nodded and reached out to shake my hand. I recalled a famous quote from Caskie Stinnett: "A diplomat is a person who can tell you to go to hell in such a way that you actually look forward to the trip."[3] Perhaps for the first time in my adult life, I really felt I lived that quote when I revealed the truth to Colton. I felt like I won a million dollars. Colton looked mesmerized and a bit emotional. I think he was picturing his granddaughter's appreciation for his grand gesture, and maybe he forgot he had an unwanted immigrant on his premises for the past two days.

I gathered my things and said goodbye to Betty. Sweet, confused Betty. As I walked to my car, I cast a wary glance at the gun store before putting that unusual environment behind me.

The drive to the airport was surreal. My heart continued to pound until I was almost over halfway there. I reflected on the past two days. I had never encountered such a politically charged environment before. When auditing, I always maintain a neutral presence but never had to be so cognizant of my facial expressions, knowing that one twitch, one raise of an eyebrow could invite potential conflict or even a life-threatening situation.

I thought about Colton and how, despite viewing the world from his very narrow lens, he still had a big heart and wanted to do something special for his granddaughter. It was a reminder that, no matter who you voted for or what you believe, we're all human and we all have people in our lives who we love. We all want to do the "right thing" in our own way.

As we journey through this book, you will learn more about the tactics I used in this life-altering situation and how empathy, awareness, and conflict management became three practical tools that helped me complete my assessment and return home, unscathed. ____

---

3 *A diplomat is a person who can tell you to go to hell in such a way that you actually look forward to the trip. Caskie Stinnett," BrainyQuote, https://www.brainyquote.com/quotes/caskie_stinnett_107330https://www. brainyquote.com/quotes/caskie_stinnett_107330.*

Summary:

- *Be aware of your response, verbal and nonverbal, at all times.*
- *In conflict, tactful information gathering can give you ammunition for a peaceful outcome.*
- *We are all human.*

Chapter 2: Son, Husband, Father, Auditor

Before I take you on a journey filled with stories, tactics, and theories, I would like to take a moment to share with you a little more about myself.

I am one of six children born to two wonderful parents. I have three older sisters and two younger brothers. We were and still are a very close-knit family. My father worked in a bank, and my mother tended to the household. We may not have been financially rich, but my siblings and I had a very rich upbringing in terms of values, culture, and togetherness. We are an emotionally synchronized family that has always been empathically connected.

I had a blessed upbringing. My parents were very loving. They still are. They never forced us to do things because it was what they thought was right. My parents were inspirational and let us be ourselves and find our own paths. They let us ask questions when we thought things were unfair, and nothing (within reason) was banned in our household.

My father gave me self-confidence. I saw a lot of parents around me asserting authority any chance they got. Not him. My father gave us the confidence to ask any question and try any task. My siblings and I felt secure in our mistakes and felt comfortable approaching my parents when we needed comfort or understanding.

One time when I was about eight years old, the power went off at our house. We had a very special flashlight that we used when there was a blackout. It was electric powered, and we only used it during special occasions. With the house shrouded in darkness, I climbed down the stairs, clutching the flashlight as it lit my path. Suddenly, I lost my footing and tumbled down the stairs. I lay at the bottom of the stairs in a crumpled heap. There, about five feet away, was the flashlight in pieces. I had broken it. I started to cry. Immediately, my father rushed into the foyer and asked if I was all right.

"I...I am okay. I broke the flashlight," I whimpered.

"Why are you crying?" my father asked gently.

"Because I broke it," I replied in between sobs.

"Forget about the silly flashlight. We can buy another. We cannot buy another Salman. You are more important."

My father's reaction was reasonable. However, I'm one of six children, and at that moment I felt like an only child. The same situation occurred when I accidentally rear-ended a bus while driving the family car. My parents' first concern was my physical and emotional condition. The second was the car.

Not that we never faced consequences for our actions. We were punished for various wrongdoings. However, my parents gave us room to explore and make mistakes as children so we could learn from them. For that, I will be forever grateful.

Growing up, I always admired people who were knowledgeable over people who had a lot of material possessions. Knowledge and intellect were far more valuable to me than expensive clothes or cars. People who were well spoken never failed to impress me. I knew that I wanted to be someone who was honest, well-spoken, and knowledgeable. I always looked for words of wisdom from seniors, leaders, and public figures.

I learned that brilliant leaders draft their values in the form of memorable mottos and live their lives adhering to them. The founder of Pakistan, M. A. Jinnah, proclaimed "Unity, Faith, and Discipline" as the secret ingredients for a successful nation. Abraham Lincoln said, "You cannot escape the responsibility of tomorrow by evading it today." [4] Gandhi said, "Where there is love, there is life." [5] These quotes and the biographies of these leaders inspired me during my search for my life's motto and values. How do I want to lead my life?

Perhaps I was too young to answer this complicated question.

After reading many inspirational books and quotes from wise men such as these, my quest eventually ended with an answer by the time I turned twenty. I identified three principles, or values, that I wanted to be the foundation of my life: honesty, balance, and consistency.

I vowed to always be honest with myself and never deceived by false accolades from others or fall prey to overconfidence. I decided never to live on either extreme, always looking to strike the right balance between individualistic and collective benefits. I realized being good once or twice would not be enough for sustained success. Whatever I did, I needed to do it consistently. I would strive for excellence. These principals remain prominent values in my life today.

I have tried to embody these values, but the paths have not

---

4 *"You cannot escape the responsibility of tomorrow by evading it today. Abraham Lincoln," AZ Quotes, https://www.azquotes.com/quote/176102.*
5 *"Where there is love there is life. Mahatma Gandhi," AZ Quotes, https://www.azquotes.com/quote/105823.*

always been straightforward. You already know my current profession, but if you were to ask young Salman what he wanted to be when he grew up, without hesitation he would answer "professional cricket player."

Cricket is one of the most popular games people in British colonies like to play. I wasn't a phenomenal cricketer with professional athlete caliber, but I was decent, and I played with great passion. My friends were cricketers, and some of my closest friends made it all the way to the professional level, becoming famous athletes in the sporting world. I feel one of my blessings in disguise was being around highly skilled cricketer friends. Just being in their company and continuously assessing my skills slowly led me to accept the fact I would never be a professional player.

Fortunately, I always gravitated toward learning new things. I attended university in Pakistan, but my thirst for knowledge was not quenched. I still had it in the back of my mind that I wanted to be a cricketer, but I also had an interest in biomedical engineering.

The thought of learning various disciplines of engineering (electronics, mechanics, robotics, control engineering, etc.) coupled with life sciences (human anatomy, physiology, biochemistry, biophysics) was the perfect blend of topics for my inquisitive mind. I enrolled in the Bachelor of Science program, majoring in biomedical engineering.

With a bachelor's degree under my belt, my mind was not sated. Socrates once said, "I know that I know nothing." That is exactly how I felt. I did not know anything yet, and I wanted to know more.

Where does one go to learn more? Graduate school. I had

three locations in mind: US, England, or Australia. After some deliberation, I made my decision. I applied and they accepted me to the University of New South Wales (UNSW) in Sydney, Australia.

It was an excellent school, and my Uncle Aftab, who was really my dad's second cousin, lived there. I admired him. He was the first person in our family (who I interacted with often) who earned his PhD. I could live with him during my studies, which would make college more affordable. Even though I knew I would not play professional cricket, I still hoped, in the back of my mind, that maybe I could develop my skills in the game and make it big. Australia is well known for cricket, and I wanted to play for the UNSW team.

Australia's open immigration system also motivated me. Immigrants could earn points for certain merits, including having a graduate degree and having an English language proficiency. These points could qualify an individual for citizenship and permanent residency in Australia.

I lived with my uncle and studied for my Master of Biomedical Engineering. True to my passion, I could also play for my university's cricket team . . . the lowest level of play, but I still got to play!

One day I was practicing fielding with my team when my coach stopped me for a quick chat. To my surprise, he explained to me the biomechanics of throwing! Coincidentally, I was taking a course on biomechanics in my masters and was relatively aware of the principles. My cricket coach was literally giving me, a biomedical engineer student, a lesson in the biomechanics of throwing a cricket ball.

It was a real "You know nothing, Jon Snow" type of moment.

If I had watched Game of Thrones back then, this quote would have summed up that experience entirely. That is how serious Australians are about cricket. I gained even more respect for my coach and team that day. I also realized three things from that conversation. One, knowing only the principles of something is not and never will be enough. Two, possibility is useless until we put them into practice. And three, I also realized once again that I'm just not cut out to play cricket on the world stage.

Instead, I graduated with my Master of Biomedical Engineering. It was time to look for a job. I made another life change. It was 2002 when I moved to Manchester, England, to live with my father's brother. My uncle always treated me and my cousin as if we were his sons. My first proper job as a biomedical engineer was at Ealing Hospital, a district general National Health Service (NHS) hospital. I was officially an adult.

I visited England a few times before, once when I was a child during the summer of 1982, once when I was only five years old, and then again during December 2000. I had a few memories of my trip in the summer of 1982. But winter 2000 was still fresh in my mind. I stayed three weeks.

During the first week, it rained every single day. It was foggy during the second week, and it snowed the third and final week. We couldn't do anything! So, in a three-week stay, I probably saw sunlight for ten to fifteen minutes, if at all. I thought England was a depressing place and figured I would never come back. But somehow, in June 2002, I returned to see my uncle. Eventually the country grew on me, and I sought permanent residency. I did not know I would end up calling that rainy, depressing place my home years later.

In those first few years in England, I had my ups and downs. In less than a year, I started a new job as a contractor for two different hospitals. I would go wherever the job sent me, for extended periods of time, feeling numb in my heart. There was no passion. There was no excitement. I would do whatever the job asked of me because I wanted to pay off my graduate school debt. I worked ridiculous hours, barely ate, and when I arrived home, I would not even turn my lights on. I just wanted to be alone, in the dark and quiet.

It took a lot of time, reflection, and enjoyable conversation with friends and loved ones, but gradually things got better. In 2003, I started working at Alaris Medical Systems. I did not fit in at first—a story I promise I will share with you later. I stayed with the company for the next five years.

Then, there was a Yorkshire lass (in Northern England, they call a lady, lass) named Kiran, who I had seen from time to time. She had beautiful, kind almond-colored eyes and long black hair. She was gorgeous. We never had a proper conversation, but I would see her around. One day I went to a family gathering with our small group of friends. At this gathering, I finally sat down and talked to her. She was brilliant, witty, and well-read.

I wish I could tell you that me and this intelligent creature hit it off, were inseparable, got married, and lived happily ever after. However, it did not exactly go that way. She wasn't particularly interested in me romantically. If I'm being honest, I was still battling residual demons, recovering from a bad heartbreak, and striving to live (though I successfully paid off my debt). I tried to court her, but she wasn't interested, so I let it go. We continued to run into each other since we shared the same family circle. When my uncle passed away in March 2005, she was there for me. My uncle's death was quite an emotional and draining experience. But time heals all pains, and, somehow, we made it through that painful time, together.

We kept in touch after that. Before Kiran went on one of her vacations, I gave her one of my favorite books as a gift. It was Dan Brown's *The Da Vinci Code*. She read it during her lengthy flight from the UK to the US. Upon her return, she thanked me for the book.

"That's the most intriguing piece of rubbish I have ever read in my life," she said.

Dan Brown unknowingly brought us a little closer. To this day, I still haven't had the chance to thank him for that favor: Maybe one day I will get my chance.

It wasn't until the summer of 2005 when Kiran reconsidered. I had worked on myself and using my faith to help me let go of the things that were weighing me down. When faced with challenges, I would tell myself, "This is a test." I would ask myself if I could sacrifice my desires to the will of God. My faith became my foundation for survival. I knew God had a better plan for me and I could not give up on myself or others. That worked for me, and I moved forward as a better man. Kiran and I started talking again, this time romantically.

One day she asked me, "What do you see your future wife doing?" I wasn't sure if it was a trick question or not, so I answered from my heart: "I want her to do whatever makes her happy. I have no expectations for her except that she does what she wishes."

That sealed the deal. After a brief engagement and blessings from both of our parents, we got married in 2006. We had two amazing children. Our firstborn son came into the world on August 8, 2008. After he was born, my wife quit her job and stayed home to raise him.

Of the many stressful milestones that happen in life, one is having a child, another is starting a new job, and a third is moving into a new home. By some luck of the draw, we completed all three life changes at the same time. It was a challenge, but an exciting one. We bought our new home, and I began working for Lloyd's Register. We welcomed our daughter into the world on September 3, 2011.

In December 2012, I shook things up again and switched jobs. We were now a family of four, on only one income, and I wanted to provide more for my family. A new opportunity with SGS (a competitor) presented itself.

I did not expect the stress and pressure that this new venture gave me. Starting a new job will always come with a little stress, but this time it was different. My key motivation to switch jobs rested on a big bonus offered to all auditors who hit their respective targets. I was traveling a lot and was incredibly busy. I spent every working hour chasing down that bonus.

Within three months I was so stressed, I was bringing my stress home. I was agitated and exhausted all the time. I had nothing against SGS or their work model. I it just did not click with my working style. It was an administratively burdened job, with insufferable amounts of paperwork. It felt like they measured my performance by how much paperwork I could complete in a day.

I was supporting my family with the promise of more money. I could not just find something I liked because this was the job that put food on the table. Then one ordinary Saturday, my life changed forever.

Summary

- *Honesty, balance, and consistency are three principle foundations of my life.*
- *My path took several directions before it led me on the journey I am still on today.*

Chapter 3: An Unexpected Path to Enlightenment

I meet strangers all the time. However, one time a stranger found me, and set me on a path I never saw coming.

Every Saturday I would take my son to Sunday school. You read that right: a Sunday school class held on Saturday. It was a community program that rented several classrooms in a school for the lessons. Saturdays were the only day available, so it became Sunday school on Saturday. It was important to me he learned good values and morals each week from a trusted institution.

The class was four hours. The school had a small break room where I set up a mobile office, so I could work and stay on site until he finished his classes. It was a nice routine, and I was very productive during those few hours I had to myself.

No good deed goes unpunished. The local community school was part of a center of excellence program. The school had to be audited. One of the assessment segments would involve interviewing randomly selected parents. The audit would determine if the school was abiding by best practices according to a globally recognized set of guidelines. They randomly selected me to participate.

It was a Saturday in March and I had just dropped my son

off when a man I had not met before approached me. He was tall, almost bald, with a small goatee on his chin.

"Are you here with your children?" he asked me with an enormous smile splayed across his face.

"Yes, my son attends Sunday school each week," I replied quickly, eager to get to the breakout room to begin my work.

"How long has your son attended this school?"

I sighed and rattled off some quick answer along with a brief apology that I could not stay and chat. I had no time for these basic questions — I would answer them when I completed the community assessment.

I figured the guy was on the panel or maybe a community coordinator, but I didn't really care to learn his role in the project. My work overwhelmed me, but I hoped to complete at least half of it while my son was in school.

I finally made it to the break room. I sat down and got busy. While I was sitting there, brow furrowed, looking at my laptop, he walked into the room and over to where I was sitting. I just could not catch a break.

"Hello there. I am Yasin Raheem, a member of the MCE community program. I'm one of the assessors in today's audit at this Sunday school," he said.

We shook hands.

"I see you're hard at work. What do you do for a living?" he asked with a smile.

Did this man ever stop smiling? I did not want to be bothered. Those four hours I had every Saturday were precious to me. It was time to get work done without interfering with my family time. I reserved my Sundays for family time. Also, I'm an introvert so chatting to strangers is not exactly my forte. What did this guy want with me?

"I'm an auditor," I replied quickly, barely glancing up from my laptop.

"That's perfect."

Perfect for what, I thought. I don't have time for this conversation.

He told me a little more about the school's audit and then presented me with a rather unique invitation.

"Why don't you join us? We have many ways you can give back to your community."

"I'm sorry, but I am too busy. I just started a new job three months ago, and I am drowning in work. I have two kids and a wife to take care of. I just need to focus on my work and not do anything extra right now."

"You should really make some time for this."

"I can't, I'm sorry," I replied hastily. I needed to get back to my work.

"It really does not take up that much time. If you are happy with the education your son is receiving, this is one small way you can contribute to the greater community."

I'm not sure why, but I reluctantly agreed to contribute to their volunteer assessment scheme. I guess I felt guilty and realized I wanted to give back and do the right thing. Moments after my submission, he dropped another annoying bombshell.

"Great! So, the first thing you would need to do is attend a three-day training to get started."

At that moment, I felt my ego light up. Did he not understand that I was an internationally recognized auditor? I did not need any training to audit a school or a community or anything. I had been doing this kind of work for years. What a silly thing to propose to a member of the International Register for Certificated Auditors. A three-day training?

"I don't need any training. I actually train auditors."

He laughed. "No, no, no. This is not auditor training. I'm sure you are very good at your job. This is something entirely different. I think you would enjoy it."

I relaxed a little. All I could think of was, why me? Why now? What did this man want from me?

He explained that the three-day training would be over a weekend. I would have to travel to Birmingham, England, and stay at a hotel. He was cryptic on the details but kept telling me how I was the perfect candidate for this training. He said those who go through the training could affect a continuous improvement program for the Sunday school and schools like it worldwide. He told me it would change both my personal life and professional career. Then he offered to pay for the entire thing—hotel, travel, and the training.

"The entire thing will be free," he assured me. "The next session is in a month."

Half of me wanted to go. I was curious. Why would this stranger invest all this time and money in me? Half of me did not want to go. What would my wife say? That would mean three days away from my family. Did I have the time at work to take off for such a venture?

My gut, my curiosity, was urging me to go.

"Okay, I will do it," I finally said.

The man's face lit up, and he requested my contact information so he could send me the details of the training.

I felt something I had not felt in a long time: excited.

A Life-Changing Workshop:
Day One

The month flew by, and finally the day for the training arrived: April 26, 2013. It was a typically cloudy day in England. I arrived at my hotel on Friday. The workshop ran through Sunday. Before we began, we had to complete a profile about ourselves to turn in to the organizers. The course leaders would review our profiles and use them throughout the workshop for various exercises and assessments.

They held the first course, a session on Myers–Briggs Type Indicators (MBTI) at a nearby community center. There were only four people in the session, so it was intimate. Dr. Sarfraz Jeraj, a clinical psychologist and qualified MBTI practitioner, led it. This was the first time I became aware of my MBTI type: introvert, intuitive, thinking, judging (INTJ).

We did not dig into the different types too deeply, but we were all tested to determine our MBTI type. Dr. Jeraj had a sense of my interests based on my written profile. He knew my type even before the test! He made us feel comfortable.

He told us a story very similar to the one about Samantha, Ellen, and Randall in the introduction of this book. He challenged us to determine which character was right and which character was wrong.

Back when I first heard this story, I wanted to know the answer. Things were very black-and-white for me then. I eagerly awaited the verdict. As I stated in the introduction, there is no right or wrong individual. They are both right, and we can perceive them both as wrong.

They slated the session for a half day. Upon dismissal, the training had piqued my curiosity even more. I did not realize people acted the way they did because of how the brain works and perceives information. With a new awareness of the distinct personality types, I saw traits of my loved ones and friends in my memories. It was fascinating!

Day Two

The next day, they held our courses at the business school within Aston University in Birmingham, UK. This time, there were 30 participants.

The conference room had tables spread throughout the space. We were told to pick any seat we like. I chose my seat and waited for others to join my table. It looked like there were about five or six people per table. My tablemates would be my group for some exercises.

"All right, everyone. I want you to grab a sheet of paper and a pen in front of you. Write two facts about yourself and one lie," the facilitator instructed us.

I grabbed the blue pen off the grey table and tapped it against my temple for a moment. Two facts and a lie—what would I say?

"After everyone writes their answers, you'll share them with your group and see if your peers can guess which statement is the lie," he said.

After a few moments, I had an idea. I wrote the following:

I have lived in Australia.

I wore jeans on my wedding day.

I'm an engineer, but if I was not an engineer, I would have been a professional cricketer.

To my surprise, my group did not get the right answer at first. They thought I was lying about my cricketer past! Did they really think I wore jeans to my wedding? The game was fun. It also allowed me to learn about my peers. It was a successful icebreaker.

Later in the afternoon we learned about different archetypes. An archetype is a term used to describe universal symbols that evoke deep and sometimes subconscious responses. They are often symbols found in literature. We learned about the archetypes: Good King, Warrior, Artist, and Guardian.

The Good King sets objectives and praises success. Kings are deliberate, precise, analytical, and logical. Warriors are inspiring, motivating, forceful, and task focused. We learned that artists are visionaries. They create change, are enthusiastic, animated, and experimental. And guardians are reassuring, supportive, empathetic, and encouraging.

Maria Pattinson, an award-winning professional theater director and practitioner with international experience as a trainer and facilitator of communication in the public and private sector, led the session. She specialized in teaching workshops on body language and soft skills. She took us on an imaginative journey.

First, we were to imagine she was a bird. This bird was an artist archetype. There was also a warrior who became king. He spent his entire life as a warrior, going to battle for his people. Like any talented warrior, he was very task focused. When he assumed his responsibilities as a king, he was very busy, deep in his duties. He became task focused and analytical. One day the bird approached him.

"Your majesty," the bird said. "I have a request. I would like to fly, but you keep me in a tiny cage."

"I'm in the middle of war, bird. I do not have time to respond to your petty request," the king replied angrily.

The king's assistant spoke up. "Your majesty, now that you are king, be considerate and listen to your followers and their requests."

"Okay. You're right. Tell the servants to fetch a bigger cage."

The servants got a bigger cage, set it up, and placed the bird inside her new and larger home. She had space to fly.

"Your majesty, thank you for the larger cage," the bird said. "But I'm afraid this is not what I meant when I made my request. I want to fly in open skies and be free. I need to smell the air and feel the wind blow through my feathers."

The king was angry and impatient.

"Bird, I gave you what you asked. You wanted to fly, and now there's adequate room for you to fly. How dare you ask me for more. You're not at war. You have nothing to do but to fly and watch the world around you. I was considerate. I gave you what you wanted, now leave me alone."

Maria stepped out of the story and asked us what happened? What was wrong?

It took a few moments, and I soon realized that the king deceived himself into thinking he was considerate. He granted the bird's request but on his own terms, not on the terms that the bird requested. He did not consider what the bird needed.

The bird, or artist, could have articulated their need differently. Artists often come up with brilliant ideas but don't articulate how they want their ideas to play out. If the bird asked to fly in unrestricted in open air, perhaps the request would be granted. However, the true lesson rests with the king's attitude.

Each archetype has some negative potentials. Good Kings rely too much on order. Warriors are very reliant on action and can appear like mercenaries or tyrants. Guardians over-nurture, like "helicopter parents." Artists often cannot articulate their needs and wants because they are caught up in expression. I thought more about the Good King and the bird.

"Have you ever felt this way? Like you were accommodating, and the other person was being ungrateful?" Maria asked us.

I absolutely had. Many, many times. This story hit me hard, right to the core. I had done this so many times to so many people. How ignorant I have become over the years!

Day Three

On the third day they divided us into two groups. We sat in a circle. Everyone had to say what they learned from the workshops and how they would use it when they returned to their families and work.

On day two, people started getting emotional, and I thought they were full of it. But now, I was changed. After the bird story, I knew I had learned a lot. I was a different man.

Many people experienced a transformation and shared stories of times they were ignorant to others' feelings. One lady explained all the things she learned and how she'd been wrong so many times throughout her life. She started to cry. I was uncomfortable. I looked down at my shoes. I didn't not know what to do or how to feel. I wanted to cry with her because I knew how she felt, but men don't cry. I sat there silent, stoic, staring at my feet.

She continued, practically confessing every wrongdoing in her own life, in between her massive sobs. I looked up at the group, carefully avoiding eye contact with her. Out of nowhere, I had a feeling.

The lady sitting next to me will get up and hug her to comfort her.

It was such a random thought to pop in my mind. Not ten seconds later, the woman to my right got up and said, "I can't take it anymore. I need to give my sister a hug."

She crossed the circle and embraced the crying participant, prompting tears from everyone

Wow, I thought. I saw and felt that happen before it happened. It could have been anyone in the room, but I had a strong intuitive feeling this woman would hug and comfort the crying woman. I was amazed by how connected we all became after just three days. It shocked me.

As the day ended, we said our goodbyes and wished each other well. We completed a survey where we selected options for future workshops. I checked "leadership development" and turned in my survey.

I arrived home around 8:30 in the evening. I walked through the door and found my wife quietly watching television, a blanket on her lap. The kids were in bed.

"How did it go?" Kiran asked me.

"I'm so sorry, Kiran," I said to her.

"For what?" she asked, her brow slightly furrowed.

"For everything. For every time I did not consider what you wanted or needed. For every time I assumed one thing, and it was another. For any time, I neglected to acknowledge your feelings. I will do better," I told her earnestly.

She cried.

"Salman, what did they do to you?"

"Nothing and everything," I said as a tear fell down my cheek.

I joined her on the couch, and we sat there, talking, and crying for at least 30 minutes. I will never forget it.

I vowed to never stop learning about self-awareness, the ego, Myers-Briggs, empathy, and all the topics they exposed me to over that weekend. I felt like it gave me a second chance at life.

My job was still stressful, but now I had a sense of why it was. The different people I interacted with on a day-to-day basis used to annoy me and stress me out. Now, I had an insight in to why they behaved the way they did. I could identify unique personality traits that made them act a certain way. It was almost fun. I had a greater awareness of the world around me, which helped me to check myself and course correct.

Back in the Classroom

A few months later, Mr. Yasin, the man that started on this life-changing path, called me.

"I heard you really enjoyed the training," he mused.

I could hear his smile through his voice. He was always smiling.

"I can't thank you enough for the opportunity to go. Thank you for seeing past my excuses and urging me to take this chance. I learned so much, and I am eager to learn more."

"That is why I'm calling. You showed interest in our leadership seminar on your professional development survey. There is an intensive five-day leadership seminar I would like you to consider.

It goes into the topics on a much deeper and personal level."

He said the course would be over two weekends. I could not afford it.

"I cannot attend but thank you for the offer."

"Why not?"

"I don't have the money."

"Just come. I can't force you, but please come. Don't worry about the money. I can cover it."

"Oh, wow, I can't accept that. That is so generous of you, but you've already paid my way once. I could not accept such an enormous gift again. Thank you just the same."

"How about this," he offered. "When you save enough money to pay for this seminar, instead of paying me back, you pay for someone else's travel, hotel, and seminar. Pay it forward. Could you do that?"

I thought about it for a moment. It seemed fair. In due time, I could save enough money for someone else to go. This option made me feel like I wasn't taking advantage of this stranger who had already changed my life once.

"Okay, I can do that."

"Great! You won't regret it."

They held the leadership seminar just outside of London. There were about 13 attendees, and it was an in-depth curriculum on conscience leadership. The attendees became so open with one another. We started the journey as strangers, and by the end of the seminar, we felt like old friends — in fact, we were like family. I learned more about how leaders should have a vision. We dove deeper into self-awareness and awareness of others. I learned that everyone has something good to offer the world; you just need to be patient and assume that as a fact.

Leadership Development: Part Two

I returned the following month for the next weekend of the training. They gave us a homework assignment: create a vision board and bring it to the seminar.

I started with the important themes in my life, chiefly enlightenment. I put up a picture of sunglasses made from handcuffs to represent how blinded I was. I had spent years looking at the world through a very limited view. I found another photo of a person being pulled into the light. This did not symbolize death, but my willingness to take my limiting sunglasses off and seek the light.

There was another image of a person trying to fly by breaking his feathers that were holding him back. Then there was a flying man, free of limiting beliefs and bathed with the warmth of the light. When we become enlightened, we receive the light, and it helps us fly to new heights.

I want to share what I have learned or understood, that helped me achieve my goals. I need to spread light to other people, so they have what they need to learn. I want to inspire people to achieve their goals, and I want to give them the tools necessary to achieve their dreams. My goals are to aspire, grow, and inspire, while living a life of honesty, consistency, and balance. We took part in several activities at this seminar. For one assignment, the facilitators split us into two sizeable groups and put us in separate rooms.

The facilitator told us to create a poster that advertises a local family picnic.

We quickly set to work, deciding on pictures to make the picnic look inviting. We wanted to use bright colors and pictures to convey happiness and a sense of warmth and welcoming. It was a beautiful poster, and we were proud of our work. The facilitators called both groups together and asked each group to present their poster.

The other poster was basic. All it said was "Picnic at Hyde Park, London, Sunday the 23rd, 2:30 p.m. Bring your own food."

Our group did not want to judge, but we thought their poster was bland.

The facilitator cleared his throat and said, "Okay, now let's talk about your poster."

We were proud! We started talking about all the creative ideas we had to make the poster inviting.

"Where is the picnic? When? Will food be provided?" a member of the other group asked us.

We were so focused on the visual aspects of the project; we forgot to put the actual details of the picnic! The other group wanted to make sure they represented the basic details before including creative elements.

"You see, we need each other to get the job done. It takes different people to contribute their ideas and talents to create a complete poster," the facilitator said.

We laughed at the obvious nature of the assignment. We also kicked ourselves for failing to include the actual details of the picnic.

Everyone has something to offer.

Applying the Lessons

The seminar was spectacular, and my understanding of leadership, motives, and actions continued to grow. I started reading more books about leadership.

The funny thing is, I don't think I read a book to completion until 2003 when Dan Brown's *The Da Vinci Code* was released. That was the first book that I read cover to cover in a few days. I'm not a fast reader; in fact, it takes me some time to finish a book. But when I read Brown's novel, I was trying to find any spare second to pick it up and continue it. I did the same with Brown's *The Lost Symbol and Inferno.*

So here I am, reading books about passion, purpose, and leadership for the first time in my life and absorbing every word on the pages. One book that made a profound impact on my life is Clayton M. Christensen's *How Will You Measure Your Life?* One chapter asks what you enjoy doing. What makes you tick? What makes you excited to get out of bed each morning?

I read those questions and took time to reflect on them. I realized that I enjoy teaching. I loved learning and sharing what I learned with others. The revelation was nice, but it was too late for me. I had my auditing career. We had a mortgage to pay. I had bills to pay, children to feed, a family to support. Did I really want to become a teacher so late in life?

I sat with that and determined the root cause of this desire. The way my previous company dealt with staff relations and day-to-day operations was more engaging. I yearned for that. Since I could not reasonably become a teacher at this point of my life, what could I do that would keep those passionate fires alive within me?

I identified ways to make my job more enjoyable. I began conducting my audits as if they were a class. For example, let's say I was performing an assessment and asked a client to show me certain documents. Instead of asking flat questions such as

"Where are these documents?" I would explain what the standard required and list the things needed on the board.

I would ask my client, "So, what do you think is missing from the document you have just shown me?" They would pause and respond with the answer and then retrieve what I needed or would realize themselves that critical information was missing. The interaction made the exchange enjoyable for me and less threatening for the client.

Rather than demand things, I got my clients to share the information willingly. When individuals recognize these things within themselves, they feel more comfortable, more confident, and more in control.

I learned all of this through coincidence. Everyone was putting me on this beautiful path of learning and awareness, even though I resisted. What if I refused to go to the training because I was too busy being stuck in my stress to open my mind to other possibilities? What if I did not go to the because I could not accept a gift (again) from a genuine human who saw something in me I did not see in myself?

I would have never taken him up on his offer if I wasn't so perplexed by his generosity. When you do something so genuine from your heart, it has an impact. People feel that impact. I know I sure did.

These learning opportunities were a grand adventure, but more adventure awaited me and my family. We remained in the UK until January 2014 when I was offered the opportunity to move to the US—Houston, Texas—and to travel all over the country performing audits on medical device companies. It was an opportunity of a lifetime and something I always wanted to do.

I talked to my wife about it. She was born and raised in the UK and had no intention of ever permanently leaving her home. However, she knew it was one of my ambitions to work and live in the US someday. She agreed, and my company packed up our belongings, arranged our temporary housing, and sent us to America. We arrived in Houston on March 18, 2014.

It was a late night, and our kids were exhausted When we entered our hotel room, our daughter cried hysterically and said, "This is not home, I want to go home." At that very moment, I felt the ground slipping under my feet. What have I done? Have I made the mistake of my life? Fortunately, all she needed was a cuddle in bed and she fell asleep.

We all woke up fresh and, thankfully, excited and in pleasant moods. It was a gorgeous spring day in Houston. The sun was shining brightly. A pleasant breeze blew by, and the temperature was around 75 degrees. I found myself humming and continuously listening to Michael Bublé's version of "Feeling Good."

The point of these stories is not to tell you how smart and clever I am. In fact, quite the contrary: I am sharing my mistakes and vulnerabilities. I want to share all the lessons I learned so far through this journey, so you don't make the same mistakes. If you find you relate to these stories or you have a story to share, please do so on my blog page. Perhaps I can learn from you, and we can all learn from each other.

Summary:

- *The generosity of a stranger opened my mind and heart in ways I never imagined.*

- *I had been like the Good King, granting requests in my life that I saw fit without considering the wants and needs of those around me.*

- *We all have something to offer. Everyone in this world has a gift, and if we don't spot it immediately, we need to discover what it is and how it can benefit others.*

Chapter 4: Tools to Build Awareness

With the training under my belt, I became more observant, keener on learning unique ways and tools to understanding people and their behaviors. I started studying people's behavior during my audits After several trainings (and dozens of books), I realized that there are innate factors that influence our behaviors. While there may well be many other contributors, I believe there are primarily three factors that influence our behaviors.

- *Personality traits we are born with*
- *Cultural values and upbringing*
- *Emotional management*

For aforementioned influencers, we will use three tools as examples for building awareness of self and others. Mind you, there are a plethora of tools and research that you can use, but in this chapter, I will highlight three that have work best for me:

- *Myers–Briggs Type Indicator (MBTI): for understanding personality types*
- *Hofstede Cultural Dimensions Theory: for understanding cultural influences*
- *Emotional Intelligence: both naturally gifted and learned through practice*

We will touch upon the first two in this chapter and the third later in the book. Let's look at the first influencer tool.

Myers–Briggs Type Indicator (MBTI)

During that life-changing training, the first day was an introduction to MBTI. The introduction blew my mind. I had heard of MBTI before but not at such an in-depth level. I could now correlate behaviors that I witnessed in others, with the different personality types. [6]

On a basic level, there are four categories with eight preferences:

Favorite World: extraversion (E) or introversion (I)

Information: sensing (S) or intuition (N)

Decision: thinking (T) or feeling (F)

Structure: judging (J) or perceiving (P)

These categories are psychological preferences we have related to different elements of our life.

We often confuse introversion and extroversion with the character traits of shy and outgoing. These two categories are more about whether you prefer to focus on your inner world or the outer world. Or what do we want to do when we are tired and need to recharge? Do we seek alone time or a social gathering?

Sensing and intuition are preferences for how we process information: observing facts and objectively viewing the surrounding information or relying on our intuition.

Thinking and feelings are preferences regarding how we decide the logic or emotion of how it feels or makes others feel.

Finally, judging and perceiving are preferences based on openness and structure. Do we make a list of things to do and break down the tasks into an even workload? Or do we keep it flexible without worrying about micro-planning?

---

6 *"My MBTI® Personality Type," The Myers & Briggs Foundation, https://www.myersbriggs.org/my-mbti-personality-type/.*

MBTI has sixteen personality types made up of these preferences. I'm an introvert (I), intuition (N), thinking (T), judging (J)—i.e., INTJ—type, though sometimes I question it.

Many of these preferences making up each personality type may conflict with one another. An awareness of MBTI will help us determine not only how our preferences affect our ideology and behaviors but also how the MBTI of others impact the way they think, act, and perceive the word.

Introvert vs. Extrovert

It is one thing to read about these personality characteristics and entirely different to see them in action. In the spring of 2015, I was conducting an audit on a medium-sized company in New York. Upon arrival, my client, Daniel, greeted me. He was a friendly man who felt confident this audit would run smoothly and his company would get the certifications needed.

I set up shop in Daniel's office, and we went over the paperwork. Whenever I asked Daniel a question, he would ramble for a few moments before getting to the answer. This happened nearly, including yes or no questions. When Daniel would ask me a question, he would pause for a half second before interrupting my train of thought with a clarification about his question. Did he think I was stupid? He did not need to spell out every inquiry.

Every time he interrupted my thinking, I had to pause even longer to plan my answer. I greeted each of his questions with a pause as I processed the question and constructed a thoughtful answer. The pause wasn't that long, but Daniel could not stand the silence. It was almost comical.

Fortunately, I had an awareness of what was going on. Daniel was an extrovert, which can also be an activist type. When extroverts hear a question, they start talking right away. Daniel was thinking of his answer while he was talking. The first few seconds of his response were irrelevant, but he always eventually answered my questions. I am an introvert, which is a reflective type.

When asked a question, introverts prefer to process it internally, analyze it, and assess their answer before responding. This process takes a few moments. If Daniel knew that I was an introvert, he would give me a few moments to answer his questions before interrupting me with a clarification. I'm pausing because I am thinking of a comprehensive response, not because I do not understand the question.

Since I picked up on the fact Daniel is an extrovert, I knew the first bits of information he offered were not what I needed. I patiently waited a few moments for Daniel to tell me the answer I was seeking.

Because of this awareness, I adjusted my behavior in these situations. Since I understand that my reflective mind requires thinking before I respond, I now inform others what I'm doing before instigating my thought process in response to a question.

I say out loud, "let me think.". This action informs the other person that, even during my silence, we're progressing. Sometimes if the situation allows, I try to think out loud, so others know what's going on in my head. I have not changed who I am and how my mind works, but this minor change makes this potentially awkward situation a lot easier to manage.

Take a moment and think about yourself. When a teacher or colleague asks you a question, what do you do? Are you an extrovert, answering right away, working the answer out as you go? Or are you more introverted, pausing to think about the question and delivering a thoughtful answer?

If you're an extrovert, take notice next time you're talking with someone. If you catch yourself interrupting a colleague or friend right after you ask them a question, try counting to ten next time before speaking again.

If you're an introvert, try the same thing and challenge yourself to speak before you reach ten. Now, you do not actually have to count in your head, since you are probably developing your response in tandem. Instead, just take a beat and challenge yourself to respond in the next few seconds.

Remember, even though an introvert may give an eloquent answer to questions, extroverts do things differently. Awareness is the key to avoid conflict and frustration. With a greater understanding, you will foster better relationships with your colleagues, strangers, and even those you love.

Sensing vs. Intuition

Another conflicting pair of preferences is sensing vs. intuition. At face value, these two preferences sound the same, but they are very different. Sensing individuals remember events as snapshots of what happened. They start with facts and form a big picture. They are highly observant and detail oriented. Objective and observable facts are their currency.

Individuals who prefer intuition may not be good at spotting the little things or details. They remember events by what they read "between the lines" about their meaning. They try to solve problems by leaping between different ideas and possibilities. They see the big picture, then find out the facts. They trust impressions, symbols, and metaphors more than what was experienced.

My brother almost lost his job because of his intuitive approach to a task. He works in Information Technology and software development as an engineer. When a technical problem arises at his work, there is a strict protocol he must follow to address the issue. The protocol is something like "If A does not work, check B. If B is malfunctioning, check C." My brother's manager was a sensing type and valued the concrete order of operations put in place for troubleshooting.

One day a problem came up and instead of following the ABC approach, my brother analyzed the situation and jumped right to the problem. He wanted to fix the issue for a customer first and follow the protocol with paperwork after. He felt the customer's needs outweighed the lengthy paperwork process that was required.

"How did you get to this point?" his boss asked him.

"I figured out the problem on my own and fixed it," my brother replied.

"But you did not follow protocol. You did not follow the steps illustrated in our process."

"But the problem is fixed. I fixed it. I had a feeling I knew what it was, and I went in there and fixed it. Now I'm completing the paperwork and making sure I record the compliance trail. We're good now."

They weren't good. My brother had to endure a long lecture on why the protocols were in place. One way to avoid this conflict would be if the manager allowed their employees to complete tasks in the way that works best for them—that is, allow them to explore problems in their own way and then analyze the result. If the result is satisfactory, and there is a complete paper trail in accordance with the procedures, then it should be acceptable. Everyone learns and completes work differently. It is not a one-style-fits-all type of world we live in.

Being intuitive may sound like a superpower, but sometimes intuitive types miss obvious things. Sensing and intuitive types balance each other out. Once again, it takes an awareness and even flexibility to let individuals carry out tasks in the manner they prefer. Both types typically want the same result; they just have unique ways of getting to that point.

Judging vs. Perceiving

The next set of conflicting preferences is judging vs. perceiving. Judging types have a very structured way of getting work done. For example, when given an extensive project, judging types may evenly break out the workload day by day, spending the allotted time to complete the project. They like organization and order. Perceiving types are the exact opposite. They might wait until the last two days to complete the project and do so in forty-eight hours. They are not rigid. Perceiving types like to wing it, in a way.

My wife and I are judging types. When we travel, we plan in advance. The night before we're set to fly, our bags are packed, and we have a firm schedule for the day ahead. We know exactly what we will do and how we will do it. Being this organized gives us peace of mind and a sense of control.

My brother-in-law, Kamran, is a perceiving type. When he travels, he does not feel that it is necessary to pack his bags well in advance. He can wake up late, pack his belongings leisurely, and even stop to ask us what is for breakfast.

My wife and I will most likely want to get on the road and have breakfast at the airport, but he will insist we have plenty of time for a bite to eat before leaving the house. This might make us anxious, but either way he will still make his flight on time.

In an office scenario, conflict can arise between a judging and perceiving type. Judging types like to methodically parse out work, while perceiving types may wait until the last minute and deliver the same high-quality results. Judging types have rigid routines, whereas perceiving types are very flexible. Both types are valuable, and they can use the strengths of each other in many ways.

If managers develop a keen awareness for these types, they can adjust their leadership style accordingly. By meeting the types where they are, and increasing awareness about personal preferences, we can keep conflict at a minimum and colleagues will feel happier, validated, and understood.

Thinking vs. Feeling

Lastly, we have thinking types and feeling types. Do you remember Randall and Samantha from the introduction? Randall wanted to spring into action, calling the police and notifying the neighbors after Ellen's apartment was robbed. Meanwhile, Samantha wanted to make sure her friend felt safe and understood. She was concerned with Ellen's emotional security. Randall was concerned with her physical security.

Thinking types are always on the hunt for the solution to the problem. They see an issue and want to tackle it and move on. Feeling types decide based on their feelings. Most of the time, they are seeking validation for their feelings before a solution to an actual problem.

My wife is a feeling type. I am a thinking type. I'm logical and technical and typically search for the solution to the problem.

When my company offered our family the opportunity to move to the US, our first few months were challenging. We were in an unfamiliar country, living in a hotel for three months. We had no credit history in the US and getting even the simplest things done was a daunting task. Every day came with more and more challenges. From the work culture to not finding our preferred groceries at the supermarket, being in a new country was difficult.

It wasn't easy for me to adjust to the US working culture, even though I was with the same company. One evening, after another frustrating day, I returned to our hotel and found my wife upset. She had lived nowhere other than the UK. She was fed up and asked me if I was too.

When I heard this, my thought process was this: my wife is frustrated and not feeling positive. Let's solve the problem by talking about some positive and future benefits we will have shortly.

"Aren't you fed up?" she asked me.

I wanted to ease her anxiety, so I tried to find a solution and I was looking for the answer to our problem.

"Well, perhaps 'fed up' is a bit strong," I replied.

"What, do you mean, 'a bit strong'?" she snapped at me, cutting me off before I could say more.

Things went south (not all the way to the South Pole, but farther than I initially imagined). I felt that I tried to help the situation, but it was too negative. Tired minds are always susceptible to misjudgment, even if you are aware of things.

The next morning, after a night of restful sleep, I realized that that the only thing my wife was seeking at the time was validation for her feelings. She just needed me to acknowledge how she was feeling and that her feelings mattered. She was not worried about the solution. She knew we had just moved and did not expect me to change that. She just wanted to be heard and understood.

It happens in the workplace all the time. Some people like to be continuously assured that their work is going in the right direction. They seek validation and revalidation. Complimenting their ongoing work goes a long way.

In contrast, thinking types might find a compliment while work is still in progress as pretentious and just lip service with no meaning. They may even find it condescending. They may think, "Hey, let me finish the work first and then comment or compliment if you like my work. Acknowledge it meaningfully (e.g., formal recognition letter, bonus, raise, etc.) rather than just a casual 'well done.'" In contrast, making a "feeling type" feel valued, even informally, can be enough.

These are just a few examples of conflicts that may occur across these preferences. However, conflicts can arise across the same preferences.

Introvert vs. Introvert

I experienced this while supervising a new auditor, Abby. She had many years of professional work experience but limited experience in the auditing world. We were on-site, conducting an audit. Soon after introductions, I knew this audit would be challenging.

Abby was shy and pensive. She looked to me not only for supervision but also to start various parts of the audit. Our client, Charles, had a similar demeanor. He was very reserved, and as I asked questions, he paused for extended periods of time. It was tense. Even though I am an introvert, I had to take an extroverted approach to move things along. Abby just would not take the lead.

We were getting nowhere. I told Abby and Charles I needed to take a break to grab some coffee. I excused myself and walked to the break room to pour myself a cup. A few minutes later, Charles walked into the room. I needed something to make him feel relaxed. He reached into the cabinet and pulled out a coffee mug. I noticed the mug had a Sheffield United logo. Sensing an opportunity, I tried to break the ice.

"How's the season going?" I asked Charles.

He paused for a second, looked at his mug, and realized what I was talking about. Immediately his face lit up, his eyes widened, and a smile spread across his face.

"Going well," he said, thankful for what he thought was common ground.

"Do you go to games often?" I asked, hoping to keep the conversation flowing.

"I have season tickets!" Charles said proudly.

"Ah, that's nice. I'm an Arsenal fan, but I just can't justify the cost," I said.

"It is worth it. I take my family from time to time," Charles replied.

We spoke about our family time rituals and how I spend my weekends with my kids. We shared a few funny stories about our, kids, wives, and life.

We made our way out of the break room and back to the office to continue the audit. Charles continued to talk about his beloved soccer team. As we walked in his office, Abby looked up from her laptop. Sensing a shift in the environment, she looked a little more comfortable.

I took control for this section of the audit. At least Charles was more open. With the tension melted, we could conduct the audit with ease. All it took was for me to find something relatable to connect with Charles on a human level. Taking an interest in him allowed him to let down his guard.

This was a case of introvert vs. introvert. Without the awareness of the personality type, two introverts can find themselves in a tense room of silence, accomplishing next to nothing.

The awareness is internal and external, - what's inside of you often appears on the outside, showing it to others. You must know how certain situations make you feel because you will subconsciously articulate your feelings through your body language.

Here is a splendid example. I was visiting my brother in Chicago. One evening they hosted a party and invited almost twenty people to their home. I was stressed - there were a lot of work pressures swirling in my mind. During the party, I sat down and started thinking about my work for the following week. I did not understand what I looked like on the outside.

"Salman, what is wrong? Are you mad at me?" my sister-in-law asked, breaking my thoughts.

"What? Oh, no, I am fine. Why do you ask?"

"Well, you look furious, and you're sitting here all by yourself."

"I was just taking a break from the crowd and thinking about my work for next week. I'm not upset with you at all. I'm sorry. You're an excellent hostess."

I wondered what people at the party thought about me. Did

they think I was some angry, brooding man? I did not realize my emotions were projecting as I indulged in my stress for a few minutes at the party.

I have a favorite meme of Mr. Nice Guy. The top image shows him smiling, and the text reads, "What I think I look like walking around." The bottom image is a picture of him scowling and the text reads, "What I look like according to everyone else."

Whether or not we like it, our body and face will reflect our thoughts and feelings and project them to the world. An awareness of this will help you do a self-check in times of negative feelings. Take a deep breath and refocus, allowing your body to reset and project a more neutral attitude. Sometimes we can accidently trigger someone's ego by projecting a "negative" emotion such as frustration or anger. Later, we will talk more talk about the ego. Our thoughts and feelings are so powerful!

But back to MBTI. There are two important things to remember. The first is that once you have an awareness of your own preferences, we cannot and must not use that awareness as an excuse for inferior quality work or the negative aspects in your relationships. Say you're a perceiving type and, when given an extensive project, you put the entire project off until the last day. If you cannot complete the project, you can't say, "Oh well, I'm a perceiving type, and that is how I work." That may be your preference, but we cannot use it as an excuse when the job is not completed. The second is that there are more tools and types available beyond MBTI. Let's look at another one:

Hofstede Cultural Dimensions Theory

The Hofstede cultural dimensions theory defines cross-cultural communication.[7] Dutch psychologist Geert Hofstede developed it. With the help of others, Hofstede established six issues that society needs to recognize, in order to organize itself. They are gauged by a scale from 0 to 100. The theory describes the effects of society's culture on the values of its members and how these values relate to behavior.

The theory identifies six dimensions.

Power Distance Index: "the extent to which the less powerful members of institutions and organizations within a country expect and accept that power is distributed unequally." Higher numbers on the index mean the country has a clear governmental order that society does not question. The rules of the nation are defined and respected.

A lower degree on the index means people in the nation question authority. They may seek democracy or an even balance of power.[8]

7 *"Compare Countries," Hofstede Insights, https://www.hofstede-insights.com/product/compare-countries/.*
8 *Felicidad García-Sanchez et al., "Chapter 2: Developing a Research Method to Analyze Visual Literacy Based on Cross-Cultural Characteristics," Global Implications of Emerging Technology Trends,*

China has a power distance index of 80, whereas Denmark has a power distance index of 18. China has a distinct and prevalent hierarchy system in place. People in Denmark, however, question authority and attempt to distribute power in a more democratic way. The US has a power index of 40, putting us in the middle of these countries in this comparison.

Individualism vs. Collectivism: This index explores what the Hofstede Insights identify as the "degree to which people in a society are integrated into groups." A society with a high index is an individualistic society. Society members focus more on "I" and less on "we," in terms of identity. Societies with a lower index are tight knit, group relationship-driven societies. [9] The US has an index of 91, whereas a country like Honduras has an index of 20. Many Central American countries are tightly integrated groups that influence relationships. The US ranks high. This country is built on individualism.

Uncertainty Avoidance Index: Hofstede Insights defines this index as "a society's tolerance for ambiguity." Societies that score a high degree in this index favor strict laws and unquestionable codes of conduct in the event of something unexpected.

Societies that have a low degree on this index are flexible, accept different ideas and tend to be less rigid. [10] China has an uncertainty avoidance index of 30 compared to 46 for the US. These countries have a higher tolerance for the unknown. However, Poland has an index of 93!

According to the Hofstede Insights country comparison tool, "Countries exhibiting high Uncertainty Avoidance maintain rigid codes of belief and behavior and are intolerant of unorthodox

eds. *García-Peñalvo and Francisco José (Hersey, PA: IGI Global), 22.*

9 *Ibid.*
10 *Ibid.*

behavior and ideas. In these cultures there is an emotional need for rules (even if the rules never seem to work) time is money, people have an inner urge to be busy and work hard, precision and punctuality are the norm, innovation may be resisted, [and] security is an important element in individual motivation." [11]

Masculinity vs. Femininity: In this dimension, masculinity is related to assertiveness, material wealth and a "society's preference for achievement." Whereas femininity is related to nurturing, cooperation, and humility.[12] If we compare the US to Sweden, we can see two very different countries from a cultural preference perspective. Sweden has an index of 5, making the country characteristic feminine.

The US has an index of 62 as a country dedicated to the American Dream, which is correlated with achievement, celebrating success, and in fact bragging (in a positive way) about personal achievements.

In contrast, societies with a low index, such as Nordic countries, are the exact opposite. These citizens don't like to talk publicly about their achievement, to keep harmony with the less fortunate population.

Long-Term Orientation vs. Short-Term Orientation: How has the past influenced the present and possibly even future challenges? This dimension correlates a society's beliefs on this very question, especially through problem solving. A lower degree of this index signifies the society cherishes traditions as a way of solving problems.

A higher degree shows the society is open to flexibility and

11 *"Country Comparison [Mexico-Netherlands]," Hofstede Insights, https://www.hofstede-insights.com/country-comparison/mexico,the-netherlands/.*
12 *Felicidad García-Sanchez et al., "Chapter 2: Developing a Research Method to Analyze Visual Literacy Based on Cross-Cultural Characteristics," Global Implications of Emerging Technology Trends,*
eds. García-Peñalvo and Francisco José (Hersey, PA: IGI Global), 22.

attacks problems circumstantially.[13] The US has an index of 26. We're just not future focused. We take things day by day. However, China has an index of 87 and South Korea has the highest at 100! These countries are continuously preparing for the long-term future.

Indulgence vs. Restraint: This dimension is exactly what it sounds like. It measures a society's tendency to take part in material wealth and gratification. A top score is a pro-indulgent society. A lower score is a pro-restraint society and they regulate indulgence by "strict social norms." [14] When comparing four countries (China, Italy, US, and Spain) the US scores the highest on this index with a 68. Behind the US is Spain with 44, Italy with 30, and China with 24. The US is indulgent.

These six dimensions measure societal influences that individuals consider throughout daily life. Based on one's cultural upbringing and exposure to each index level in each dimension, individuals' worldviews are shaped accordingly.

I experienced this firsthand while conducting an audit for a company. I liaised with the site quality manager, Stacey, and we agreed to meet at 9:30 a.m. on the first day of the audit. Unfortunately, a tremendous storm hit our area the morning of the meeting. Stacy started receiving excuses from senior managers claiming they could no longer attend. Their CEO could not make it in time, so he put one of the office managers in charge for his portion of the audit. Hours later, we received a call from their marketing manager. She too would not make it. She designated her associate to take her place.

Most of their senior managers could not attend in person. We

---

13 *Ibid.*
14 *Ibid.*

waited for fifteen minutes in case any stragglers decided they could make our meeting. Around 9:35 a.m., we began. Then, at 9:47 a.m., one of their newly hired senior technical managers, Leda, arrived.

"Is this the auditing meeting?" she asked as she scanned the room.

"Yes," the office manager replied. "Have a seat."

"Where is the CEO? Where is our marketing manager?" Leda asked us.

"They could not make it because of the weather," the office manager said.

"But we can't start the meeting without them," Leda insisted.

"They designated people to serve in their place," Stacey offered.

"Okay, but why did you start the meeting without me?"

"We thought you were stuck in the nasty weather," Stacey said, her voice shaking slightly.

"Okay, so you don't need leadership anymore. I get it!" Leda said. And with that, she walked out and slammed the door shut.

I jumped at its impact. Stacey was an inhale away from tears. We looked around at each other, stunned.

"Let's continue," I said because I was unsure what else to say.

After the meeting, I went to find Leda and apologized for the way things went.

"It is not your fault," Leda said. "The entire process is off."

She explained to me what she meant. After that conversation, I figured out that Leda originated from a Turkish society with a high-power distance index. In her country, the hierarchy is in place for a reason and without question. She was used to leaders calling the shots. In her mind, based on her cultural organization, she felt that our meeting could not take place without our CEO and senior management in attendance. Any replacements were merely subordinate. It was a teachable moment, for sure.

The more I researched the various Hofstede dimensions, the more I saw them play out everywhere. Take China, for example. In business culture, relationship management is pivotal to any business deal. That is to say that the business parties must get to know each other on an almost personal level before a business deal is closed. Prospective business partners socialize beforehand, mostly over drinks, before making key business decisions.

The more you know that these dimensions exist, the more easily you will see how cultural and societal structures influence personality traits and behaviors. It is almost like learning a new language.

It is also important to understand that MBTI and the Hofstede cultural dimensions are not the only personality indicator tools out there. There are several other psychometric tests available, such as the Four Temperaments Test and The Big Five Model of Personality. Try them out. You can never learn too much about yourself and the world around you.

Summary

- *There are three factors that influence our behaviors:*
  - *Personality traits we are born with*
  - *Cultural values and upbringing*
  - *Emotional management*
- *Three tools to build awareness are:*
  - *Myers–Briggs Type Indicator (MBTI): for understanding personality types*
  - *Hofstede Cultural Dimensions Theory: for understanding cultural influence*
  - *Emotional Intelligence: both naturally gifted and learned through practice*
  - *There are many other tools you can use to build awareness of self and others and measure factors that influence our behaviors.*

Chapter 5: Examining the Ego

With a greater understanding of personality types and the behaviors associated with each, it is now time to look at the self once again. Over the years, I have learned a lot about the ego. While Sigmund Freud may have coined the term and respective theory, I believe the ego is an innate feeling of self-importance. It can be stubborn, and it can be self-righteous. The ego can be triggered, and we can pacify it. It can also be complicated.

Whenever we function from our real self, joyful. The most creative and constructive contributions to life come from our inner self. Everything that is great and generous, everything that is life-expanding, beautiful, and wise, comes from the inner self or real self. I cannot emphasize this often enough, even in our meditations. Trying to understand this truth, not only with our mind but with our feelings, is essential. Let me explain.

The ego plays an important role in our lives. Without it, we would lack a sense of self-importance. We might find our existence meaningless.

However, the ego, when unchecked, can be a dangerous thing. The psychological understanding of ego is paradoxical, and we must strike the right balance. Ego and self-esteem are vehicles to achieve our goals.

They are like riding a horse, but we should control the horse, not the other way around. We should lead the horse where we want to go. In this chapter, we will discuss how to strike the right balance and to control our horse (ego).

As I've said, we need our egos (our horse), but we need to keep our egos under control. It is much easier said than done. In this book, we're only focusing on unchecked and negative effects of ego. When we are not in control of our egos, we put ourselves on a fictional pedestal. If someone or something threatens to knock us off that pedestal, we get defensive and indignant.

Or we at least feel defensive. We might not act on our defensive feelings, but there is no denying that feeling of frustration.

Frustration begins with a feeling that a person, group of people, or system is not treating you fairly. You feel as if you deserve better than what is happening. This is the ego at work. When we feel frustrated, often it is because we feel we are better and deserve better.

When our ego is dormant, we are calm and less frustrated. When our ego is triggered, we become frustrated. This frustration does not help us. It can cause detachment, negativity, and stress.

Triggers

When our ego lights up, something or someone triggers that response. There are many triggers out there, including action, facial expression, body language, and tone of voice.

Triggers can frustrate us.

Let's look at how body language can trigger the ego. A friend of mine told me a story about two individuals, Sydney, and Harrison, who are colleagues. They work for an insurance company in the claims management department. Their job is to collect information from clients who are making claims and prepare reports for the claims adjuster. Sydney worked for the company for five years. Harrison worked there for a little over a year. Mostly, Sydney and Harrison worked well together. Occasionally, they bumped heads.

One afternoon the two of them were working together to compile a report. Harrison noticed a few client records that seemed off. He looked over them several times and knew he had to speak up.

"Syd, these don't look right," Harrison said.

"What do you mean? The client said they docked the boat during the hurricane, and it suffered damage. It is a pretty black-and-white," Sydney replied.

"I'm not so sure. It says here the client had his boat docked to the left of the pier, but I looked into it, and you can only dock boats to the right of that pier," Harrison said.

"He probably mixed up his directions. We'll let the adjuster deal with it."

"I really think we should double-check with the client, Sydney."

He rarely used her full name in conversation. Sydney looked up from her computer.

"Harrison, I don't appreciate you butting in. I have been at this much longer than you. These things happen. Let it go," Sydney chided.

Harrison sighed and walked back to his desk. He was determined to figure out any discrepancies before they sent their report to the adjuster.

Sydney knew that Harrison might be right, but she did not want to admit it. The way he spoke to her, using her full name, acting out of assertion, made her feel threatened. Sydney felt as if

Harrison did not think she knew how to do her job. She had four more years of experience under her belt. She did not want to be challenged by a new employee. She did not want her boss to hear a younger employee challenging her. It had triggered her ego.

Harrison challenged Sydney's own infallible perception of herself. She did not want to admit to him or herself that she might make a mistake. Instead of recognizing this, she wanted to protect her ego. Thus, she failed to give Harrison the benefit of the doubt. She failed to understand that he wasn't coming from a position of power but a legitimate concern regarding the work they were doing, so Sydney dismissed him.

A few days later, the pair found out the client had been lying about several aspects of the insurance claim. Harrison was right.

Being the more senior employee, Sydney was questioned heavily and ultimately took responsibility for the error. Harrison was not in trouble, but they gave Sydney a warning. She later apologized to him. The entire mishap could have been avoided if Sydney was in touch with her ego! It all starts with awareness. She thought she was protecting her senior status, but she ended up damaging her credibility instead.

It Happened to Me

If you recall, I did something similar. Remember when I met Mr. Yasin in the break room of my son's Sunday school? When Mr. Yasin told me about a three-day training, I would need to attend to be a part of the auditing project. I was angry. I could not believe this stranger thought I needed auditing training when I was a well-known auditor who trained other auditors.

Thankfully, Yasin sensed how I felt and managed the situation impeccably. He disarmed my ego by acknowledging my credentials and telling me the training was for something different, reassuring me he thought I was good at my job. My ego was tamed, and I could listen to what he was offering.

Our ego can be the loudest voice in our heads. This makes it difficult to hear what the other person is trying to share with us. We get wrapped up in trying to please the ego—ready with a defensive retort or clarification—that we cannot miss the valuable information being presented to us. Look at Sydney: if she had just listened to Harrison, maybe she would not have gotten in trouble.

Think about the last time you disagreed with someone. Did you get defensive? What were the moments leading up to that disagreement? Did they say or do something to upset you? Now, why were you upset in the first place? Really think about it. It is likely they threatened your ego at some point, and you felt the need to fix that feeling instead of addressing the situation at hand.

Let's Talk More about Triggers

Facial expressions and body language can also trigger our egos. I see this happen with clients during my audits. There was a time when I was auditing a client in Copenhagen. My client, Sven, was a very tall and thin man with a higher-than-expected pitched voice. He was balding and in his mid-forties.

Sven had this essence about him where he wanted to make sure he pleased everyone he met. He seemed like he needed to always do the right thing, present the right information, and deliver what they requested on the first try. Part perfectionist and part people pleaser, Sven makes for a great client to work with.

It was a warmer-than-usual day in mid-July. After some introductory chitchat, I began my order of operations for day one of my audit. Sven was eager to provide me with whatever I requested. This behavior was not only true for the audit, but personally. Need more coffee? Sven would be back in a jiffy. Hungry? Sven brought pastries for the staff this morning. Would I like one?

"You're sweating, Mr. Raza," Sven said. "Let me see if I can turn the air conditioning up a few more notches to make you more comfortable."

That day, I had a massive headache, so I was not in the game. I was thinking about my family and the plans for my son's upcoming birthday party. There was a chance I would be in Windsor, outside of London, for his birthday, despite requesting vacation time for a few days so I could be home to celebrate. I hadn't slept much the night before and, overall, I just felt nauseous. I think it was part stress and part illness but wasn't sure.

My symptoms made me sweat and hunch over. I tried to be pleasant, but it was much easier for me to stay quiet and say as little as possible. What I did not realize was that my headache was causing me to wince ever so slightly. This seemingly involuntary spasm of my face occurred every time Sven spoke. Thinking back, it may have been his high vocal tone!

"Is there something wrong, Mr. Raza?" Sven asked me.

"No, no, everything is fine. You have all the required documents in order," I told him.

I winced. It is almost comical now, but I did not understand that my body language was triggering him. My discomfort ignited a sense of concern within Sven. He was now suspicious of me, my work, and the audit. I could tell he was panicking.

"Everything is in order so far. I have a slight headache, that is all," I tried to reassure him.

"I can see if anyone on my team has some aspirin. Would you care for some?" Sven asked, as if offering me medication would assure a successful audit.

The audit would already be successful. Sven was a no-stone-left-unturned client.

"No, thank you. I try not to take medicine unnecessarily. Perhaps it is a side effect of dehydration. Let's just continue with our work," I said and drank more water.

Sven eased up a little, but I could sense him watching me, looking for clues of something unfavorable. Fortunately, we could complete our day's work an hour early, and I returned to my hotel to rest and try to get well.

It was Sven's nature to look for signs of displeasure or discomfort and fix them immediately. Though innocent and helpful, Sven's ego also made him feel like a supreme helper and aide. When he picked up on my body language, he felt threatened. When I told him about my headache, his ego eased up and he calmed down a little. I had neutralized the threat.

When you know what your own ego triggers are, you develop a greater sense of what triggers others. Consider this knowledge to be a secret weapon. Using it will help you mitigate conflict.

Taming the Ego

How do we tame our ego? Well, beyond the ever-important awareness, we can build upon that foundation. When you notice yourself feeling angry or defensive, stop for a moment. Do an inventory of your feelings. Ask yourself, "Why do I feel angry?" or "Why does this upset me?" Pause and think before reacting. By processing these feelings, you'll give yourself a buffer of time to contemplate your next step instead of reacting impulsively. Take a deep breath and let the feeling go.

Think about the ground. The ground takes in everything: rain, sunshine, the stomping of feet, you name it. We plant seeds in the ground, and it takes everything so humbly. The ground does not really move; it is a passive energy. However, through that passive energy, a seed is nourished and breaks through the surface into the light. The ground absorbs the energy from the sun, the rain, and the atmosphere and produces a beautiful thing. The ground handles everything thrown at it with grace and humility.

It is through humility that we can conquer the ego's desires. We must harness our own passive energy. It takes humility, patience, and rational thought. The ego is not rational. The ego is impulsive. The ego wants you to think you are superior, and any interaction threatening that thought will cause negative feelings to stir.

However, when our self-interest takes a back seat in this car ride called life, we are more in tune with ourselves and those around us. When our ambition comes from a place that is less self-serving and more other-serving, we start to master our ego.

Remember, even if you do not get defensive, you do, in fact, feel defensive.

One time, I was driving from Winston-Salem to Charlotte, trying to catch a flight. As I was driving, I got stuck behind a car that was driving slowly in the passing lane. Prior to this encounter, I was speeding a little I was in a hurry and needed to get to the airport. I crept up behind the slow car. I could see the driver was talking on a cell phone!

I abruptly swerved into the right lane to pass the car and return to the fast lane. Moments later, flashing lights went off on the top of the car. I had just bullied a police car with my impatient road rage. The officer pulled me over.

Even though what the officer was doing was not right by any stretch of imagination (he should not have been in the passing lane, driving slowly while talking on his cell phone), I knew what I did was wrong.

The officer came to my window and started shouting at me. He asked what I thought I was doing and accused me of driving like a lunatic. His voice was loud, and his tone was escalated.

He should not have been talking on his cell phone while driving, but I was not about to address that with him. Instead, I apologized. I told him what I did was wrong, and that I was very sorry. I was earnest, humble, and kept repeating my apology.

Gradually the yelling subsided. With each apology and respectful sentence, the officer de-escalated. A minute later he was speaking to me in a regular tone. He checked my license, registration, and insurance, and they were all in order.

He let me off with a warning. No ticket! Truthfully, I think this was because he did not have evidence that I was speeding. I was behind him when I was driving a little over the speed limit. During the inciting incident, I was going the proper speed.

The point is, I triggered and disarmed his ego. But if I argued and reminded him of his mistakes, he would have found reasons to give me a ticket or subjected me to a grossly disproportionate police response to my simple action. We all make mistakes, and when both sides have made a mistake, it is best to apologize for your own.

Assess where you are internally and try a humble path. Humility is a magnificent tool to pacify any situation. Whether or not we like it, it works and helps calm not only our own ego but the ego of others.

Now, I'm not saying to apologize for everything. If you are innocent and there is not any doubt that you have done nothing wrong, then respectfully stand your ground. But if there is even the slightest chance you did something wrong; it is best to own up to it.

Let It Go

There are a few variations of an old story about two people. For our purposes, we'll say the story is about a disciple and a wise man. The wise man asked the disciple to grab two pails and fill them with water. After the disciple does this, the wise man said they must travel to the top of the mountain with the water. The wise man did not explain why but told the disciple he must do the task. The disciple obeyed, filling the two buckets with water, and grabbed the handles, ready to make the lengthy trip.

As they ascended the mountain, the disciple quickly grew tired. The buckets of water were heavy, and his arms hurt. He complained to the wise man, asking him why they were doing this. He just wanted the journey to end.

After many hours, they reached the top of the mountain. The wise man asked him if he enjoyed the journey. He asked him what he liked the most about the landscape. The disciple was angry and exhausted. He ignored those questions and asked the wise man what he wanted him to do with the buckets of water.

"Dump them out," the wise man told him.

"You want me to dump them out? After I carried them all the way up here?" the disciple asked incredulously.

"Yes," the wise man replies.

With a touch of sass, the disciple poured out the buckets.

"Now what?" he asked the wise man.

"Now you can enjoy the journey as we go back down."

On their way back, the wise man asked the disciple what he saw and felt. The disciple described the beautiful scenery and said he felt great joy. He said he could feel every single visible and invisible beauty around him. He was so surprised that he did not see any of it when they were climbing up. The journey could have been much easier and enjoyable!

The wise man quietly joined the disciple's contemplation. "When you carry resentment, anger, and frustration, it will weigh you down. You will lose sight of the journey and the surrounding beauty. You become focused on negativity and those feelings alone."

The disciple comprehended.

"But if you let go of these things, your load becomes much lighter. You enjoy the journey and admire the landscape. You are free," the wise man told him.

We may not be carrying actual buckets of water around with us everywhere we go, but we carry those negative feelings and frustrations with us. These things weigh us down. The ego, when active can weigh us down. If we let go, we're able to enjoy more and live a beautiful, full, and joyful life.

Ajahn Brahm, a British-Australian Theravada Buddhist monk, has given many talks about letting go. In one talk, "Four Ways of Letting Go," [15] he shares a story about a stick. A stick is only heavy if you are carrying it. When you put the stick down, it is no longer heavy. As an exercise, try finding a stick in the forest and carve one or two of your burdens on it. Toss the stick as far as you can.

---

15 Ajahn Brahm, *"Four Ways of Letting Go," Buddhist Society of Western Australia, https://bswa.org/teaching/ four-ways-letting-go-ajahn-brahm/.*

You cannot be burdened by what you do not carry.

Another way we can strive to let go is to pause and ask ourselves, "Is it really that bad?"

I once had a colleague who was habitually late for work. She would come in only a few minutes late here and there, but she was always late. She blamed traffic, her alarm, the weather, pretty much anything she could other than herself. Her direct supervisor did not hold her accountable because he was late a lot. This went on for several months until her supervisor called her into his office for a meeting.

Twenty minutes later, she emerged from the office, her face red and her brow furrowed.

"I can't believe it," she said as she walked past my desk.

I did not want to get involved, but I could tell she expected someone to respond to her statement. I paused from my work.

"What's wrong?" I asked.

"The audacity. I just got a written warning for tardiness," she said angrily. "He of all people should not be calling me out for being late."

Her ego was lit. She felt she deserved aa pass on her lateness because her supervisor was also late. She believed her excuses were valid reasons that justified her tardiness. She felt like they wronged her.

"What did you say?" I asked her.

"Nothing. I wanted to call him out, but I did," she replied. "I said I would do better and apologized."

She did the right thing, despite her ego being wounded.

"Go back to your desk. Take a deep breath. Think to yourself, is it really that bad?" I told her. "Did you get fired? Did he yell at you or humiliate you in front of your colleagues?"

"No," she said and walked away.

I could tell she was still agitated but less agitated than when she first approached me. It would take time, but eventually her ego would recover, and she could get back to work without carrying with her all those feelings from the confrontation.

It really takes time, practice, and a keen awareness of outside triggers and yourself. However, when we tame our egos, we can eliminate unnecessary frustration in our lives. We can take careful steps to avoid triggering others, paving the way for peaceful and meaningful relationships.

Summary:

- *The ego is an innate feeling of self-importance.*
- *Body language, tone of voice, and misinterpreted social signs can trigger our egos.*
- *Awareness of individual triggers is how you tame the ego.*

Chapter 6: Triggered Egos and How to Tame Them

With a greater understanding of the ego, let's explore why it is triggered so easily. There are a lot of psychological and sociological reasons behind it, but what it boils down to is that we, as humans, have a fear of being judged. Okay, maybe all of us are not "fearful" of being judged, but we can all agree we disliked It.

A Squeaky-Clean Image

We want to believe we are smart, eloquent, and all-around decent people. When we make a mistake, be it intentional or not, many of us resort to excuses, explanations, and playing dumb. At an early age, we're taught what we should avoid, and we must strive to do our best in all things. As we grow older, we learn the value of teachable moments brought on by mistakes. We also learn that in life, mistakes are inevitable.

When we make a mistake and someone points this out, it sets off feelings of guilt deep within our core. Sometimes shame likes to accompany guilt. After these feelings come to pass, we feel anger. We question ourselves and play the offending scenario over and over in our heads. We want to believe we are infallible, but as we've heard many times over, "to err is human." The pursuit of perfection manifests insecurity and defensive behavior. Sometimes, it may also inspire deceitful behavior.

Imagine this scenario: Kevin is four years old. His mother just made a batch of sweet-smelling chocolate chip cookies. Kevin really wanted a cookie, but it would be dinner time in 20 minutes and those cookies were for dessert. Kevin's mother told him he couldn't have a cookie until after dinner. Kevin was disappointed and couldn't stop thinking about the cookies. The delicious morsels were sitting in the open, on the counter, just begging to be eaten.

Kevin's mother went downstairs to the basement to fold some laundry. Kevin, eyeing the cookies, decides he just couldn't wait and wanted to eat one. He cautiously walked to the counter and took a small cookie from the corner of the cooling rack. He ran into his playroom and devoured it. To him, that devious act was worth the instant gratification it provided. Afterall, Kevin is only four.

When Kevin's mother returned to the kitchen she glanced at the counter and counted the cookies. When she realized one was missing, she called Kevin into the kitchen. Reluctantly, he obeyed. She questioned him, but he denied taking the cookie. He said his six-year-old sister must have wandered in the kitchen and taken one. He claimed to be playing with his trains the whole time.

Kevin's mother knew he is lying, and Kevin ultimately was punished. He lied because he did not want to get in trouble. He made excuses and tried to get out of the situation. He feared the repercussions, which were inevitable because he made a choice and it was the wrong one.

Caught with Cookies as Adults

What does this look like when an adult does the same thing? Instead of cookies, it may look like poor business decisions.

In one of my favorite books, *How Will You Measure Your*

Life? Clayton Christensen, James Allworth, and Karen Dillon share with us an excellent example:

Nick Leeson, a 26-year-old trader famously brought down the British merchant bank, Barings, in 1995. He racked up $1.3 billion in trading losses before being detected, and knew he was making bad decisions He now speaks eloquently how marginal thinking led him down an inconceivable path. [16]

His demise began with a small error that he did not want to admit to. He made a bad trade deal. Wanting to protect his own "infallible" image, Leeson dug a metaphorical hole equivalent to a career grave. He covered his error by hiding the loss in another trading account. Christensen, Allworth, and Dillon write, "[Leeson] made a series of bets to pay the losses back—but rather than paying off, they made the problem worse." [17]

They arrested Leeson in Germany after he ran from his home in Singapore. Barings declared bankruptcy. Twelve hundred employees lost their jobs, including Leeson's comrades. They sentenced Leeson to six and a half years in a Singaporean prison.

Why could not he just admit his error? Honesty would have saved him a world of heartbreak and many jobs. He was so fixated on becoming rich and gaining success that he would sacrifice the invaluable treasure of trust and integrity to get there.

This example illustrates my point. Think about your own life. Have you ever told a lie — either a major lie or a white lie — to get out of a situation where you made a mistake? What about making excuses?

---

16 Christensen M. Clayton, James Allworth, and Karen Dillon, How Will You Measure Your Life (New York: HarperCollins, 2012), 187.
17 Ibid.

Vulnerability

We need to learn to accept that mistakes are okay. Mistakes can be our greatest teachers. We do not have to lie or make excuses. The best thing we can do is own our faults in times of error. When we say, "I'm sorry, I made a mistake," we become humble and vulnerable.

Vulnerability opens us up. It allows us to be open to things such as teachable moments, self-awareness, and awareness of others. Vulnerability gives us the opportunity to be perfectly flawed and human. Vulnerability is one of the special things that can calm down a triggered ego.

I have learned that vulnerability is a key element in my work with auditing. There have been many occasions where I work with a client, and they are upset or flustered with the audit. Nonconformance issues are the primary trigger points. No one wants to hear they have a nonconformance.

When they do, I see them exhibit behaviors like our friend Kevin. Many times, they make excuses or try to explain to me why the situation is the way it is. They hope I will see their side and not issue a nonconformance.

I let them talk, and I listen patiently. Then I offer something that I know some of my colleagues do not: I share a few of my own mistakes with the client. I will tell them of a time I was on the other side of the auditing relationship and I made a mistake. I share with them the anger I felt when I was told that I did something wrong. I channel my empathy so the client can see that I have been in the same position they are. I do not want my clients to think I, or my company, are "above" them.

If that does not work, I try another tactic: I channel their humanity. I once told a client that if I did not write the nonconformance, I would lose my job. I asked them if they wanted that. They said no. I told them I understood where they were coming from. I could see their ego disarm right before my eyes.

It works nearly every time. As I share more about myself and my own vulnerabilities, I can sense the foundation of common ground. People soften. They calm down. It is a beautiful thing. Vulnerability can disarm the other person. Think of it as if you are saying, "You are only human. I am too."

You don't have to be an auditor to try this. Everyone can take their own mistakes and failures and use them to level the playing field in daily interactions. The key is to be genuine. Really choose those challenges you've faced and mistakes you have made that apply to the interaction.

Saying, "I know how you feel" or "I have been there," is not enough. Those phrases have become overused and meaningless, if not patronizing. It does not matter if you know how the other person feels. You must find examples to show that rather than just tell them. Using examples gives genuine meaning to the foundation you're trying to establish. You will have to be a little vulnerable.

Vulnerability can disarm, but let's revisit this notion of mistakes. Mistakes are our greatest teachers. Did you know how the cleaning agent 409 got its name? It took the company 409 attempts to get the formula right! We learn so much by doing, and we learn even more by failing. We often think mistakes are bad and cannot see the good that comes from them. Sometimes, it is our failures and disappointments that put us on the path we're destined to travel.

Disappointments and Destiny

The 2011 movie I comes to mind. It is one of my favorite movies. It stars Matt Damon as politician David Norris and Emily Blunt as contemporary dancer Elise Sellas. Norris is a wildly successful and popular politician. He meets Elise, and the pair inevitably fall for one another. But not everything is what it seems. A group of men are determined to keep them apart. The men of the Adjustment Bureau will stop at nothing to control David's path. What appears to be fate are premeditated cause-and-effect experiences. The Bureau makes things happen at very specific moments to ensure the outcome they want.

Focused on his own agenda, David does not see what is happening around him. At least, not at first. The message is simple: sometimes we get so limited in our pursuit for something that we miss the signs around us. David eventually figures it out.

It got me thinking. Sure, there is no Adjustment Bureau in our lives, controlling our every thought or action to align with a premeditated outcome. However, what if our mistakes lead us where we're supposed to go? What if those failures we dwell upon and feel shame about ultimately make our lives better? We're so focused on what we want, we forget to pick up the lessons we need.

This happened to me many times. After I earned my master's degree in Australia, I was looking for the next step in my life. At the time, my best friend worked in a paid scholarship program at the University of Connecticut.

Another friend of mine got into this same program with the help of my best friend. They wanted me to apply for the program. After some convincing, I finally agreed.

I began the admissions process with great enthusiasm. I studied for my GRE testing and filled out the applications. I put a lot of effort to get in. I pictured my life in America, living, working, and studying in Connecticut. This would be the next step in my life plan. If my friends could get into the program, then so could I. I wanted this to work out.

After a lot of effort and anticipation, I finally got the answer I had been waiting for. But it was not the answer I wanted. I did not get accepted into the program. My life plans were completely scrapped. I wasn't sure what to do. So, I applied for Australian citizenship. I thought I had plenty of points in my favor, including my advanced degree with a focus in biomedical engineering. Except there was a discrepancy regarding the amount of points offered for my degree. Because of the numeric weight my degree had, I was a measly five points short of citizenship eligibility. Five points!

So there I was, unable to permanently stay in Australia. I could not go to the US as a student of the University of Connecticut program. I had an enormous debt from graduate school that I needed to pay off. I spent years studying biomedical engineering. What was I going to do with this degree?

I became utterly depressed. I felt defeated, and I felt like a failure. I had spent so many years in school studying to become someone, and it felt like no one wanted me. I wasn't good enough for anything.

It was this chain of events that led me to England, where I lived with my uncle and began my first "proper" job. I met my wife in England. I started my family in England. It was a job in England that gave me the opportunity to move to the US. All these things would not be possible if I got into that program my friends got into or if I had earned Australian citizenship. My life would be vastly different, and possibly not for the better.

I keep in touch with my friends who attended that program that I so desperately wanted. They are doing all right, but now my best friend wants to find a way into my field of work. Years ago, I would have given anything to be like him. Now, it looks like he wants to be me! (Okay, he does not want to be me, but he really would like to be in my field).

Thanks to my setbacks, my life is so much richer than it could have been. My beautiful family and steady job serve as daily reminders that I'm doing well.

Emergent and Deliberate Strategies

Clayton Christensen defines what is called emergent and deliberate strategies. An emergent strategy is one that is born out of trying to follow a specific plan but being led in a different direction. A deliberate strategy is one that follows a specific.

In his freshman year of college, Christensen decided he wanted to become the editor of the *Wall Street Journal*. His deliberate strategy was to major in economics and business to distinguish himself within a journalism niche, instead of majoring in journalism. Having a specific field of study would take him out of the generalist field and create opportunities as a business writing and editing candidate. This decision led him to pursue his MBA at Harvard.

He applied for a summer position with the *Wall Street Journal* but was rejected, so for the time being he took an internship at a consultant firm. By taking this job, he inadvertently submitted to an emergent strategy. In Christensen's mind, he would gain some experience firm which would look good on his resume for his ultimate career goal. He did not expect to fall in love with the job, but he did.

This happened several times throughout his life, and while he's written books, he never secured that editor role with the *Wall Street Journal*. He found his path through emergent strategies, one right after the other. He found love and fulfillment, passion, and purpose, on those roads he thought would eventually lead to that editor position.

I see parallels in Christensen's story and my own. I wanted to be an Australian citizen, but that did not pan out. I wanted to enter the University of Connecticut program, but that did not work out. I always wanted to work in the US, and that panned out, but it took time.

We can find stories of emergent and deliberate strategies in just about every sector in life. In *The Alchemist* by Paulo Coelho,[18] a young shepherd named Santiago goes on a quest to find treasure at the foot of the Egyptian pyramids. Santiago meets an Alchemist where he learns how to follow his heart.

Throughout his journey, Santiago discovered all types of riches in love, knowledge, and self-awareness. These treasures far outweighed the ones he was seeking. After finally finding the treasure in a church from his dreams --which inspired his journey -- he returned it to the Alchemist and consequently was reunited with a woman whom he had met and fell in love with during his quest. After the lessons he learned from his travels, the nonmaterial treasures now mattered more to him

A more modern example is Brian Acton. [19] Acton worked for

18 Paul Coelho, The Alchemist (New York: HarperCollins, 1993).
19 WhatsApp Founder Brian Acton Was Rejected by Facebook for a Job," NewsComAu, February 24, 2014, https://www.news.com.au/finance/business/whatsapp-founder-brian-acton-was-rejected-by-facebook-for-a-job/news-sto

Yahoo and eventually applied to work at Facebook at the height of its growth. They rejected him. But because of their rejection, Acton eventually cofounded the popular chat application WhatsApp. He ended up selling the app to Facebook for $19 billion dollars! What if they had given him a job opportunity at Facebook? Would WhatsApp even exist?

A bunch of employers, including Kentucky Fried Chicken, rejected Jack Ma.[20] According to Ma, they interviewed twenty-four people for a position at the fast-food chain. Twenty-three people got the job. A fast-food position just wasn't in his cards. Instead, Ma learned a lot about the internet and became a Chinese internet mogul, and the richest man in his country. He's the founder of Alibaba, China's internet marketplace.

Fail Gloriously

When we fail, it is important to fail gloriously. That failure might just point us in the right direction. The challenge is that hindsight is 20/20. We don't realize the setbacks, rejections, mistakes, and failures in our lives will eventually lead us to where we're supposed to be all along. In that moment of rejection, failure, or pain, we feel ashamed and angry. We have a challenging time seeing the positive in what feels like an impossibly never-ending negative situation. Yet we must take these things and embrace them as blessings. If you don't believe in blessings, then at least see them as signs, a prompt to look for new clues, new opportunities, new possibilities, and new ventures.

This is true for our failures too — those mistakes we beat ourselves up over. Striving to be perfect all the time is a recipe for

ry/2db6f3d007e399a1edc02a29ddda5cc8.
20 Madeline Stone and Jillian D'Onfro, "The Inspiring Life Story of Alibaba Founder Jack Ma, Now the Richest
Man in China," October 2, 2014, https://www.businessinsider.com/the-inspiring-life-story-of-alibaba-founder-
jack-ma-2014-10.

disaster and will generate an overactive ego. Do not fear mistakes. When we are not scared of making mistakes, we become calm and feel secure in our hearts and our minds.

Feelings of calm and security ground us and allow us to embrace an essence of control. This leads to positive and tolerant behavior. We're no longer interacting in a manner where we get defensive at the slightest tickle of our ego. Our self-confidence grows, and positivity infects those around us.

Nobody is perfect. And honestly, why would you want to be? You would miss out on the valuable lessons your mistakes and failures teach you. Perfection would rob you of the opportunity to share the lessons with those around you.

It's for the Best

We must change our mindset to realize that sometimes our mistakes, failures, and disappointments are for the best. I have a great story I tell my son. He loves the story so much; he now quotes it in certain situations.

There once was a powerful king who lived in a faraway land. His name was King Kalif. He had a trusted assistant minister named Barnabas who served as his primary advisor. Whenever conflict or disappointment would occur, Barnabas would say, "It is for the best." King Kalif never understood why Barnabas loved that phrase so much. He must have said it hundreds of times.

One day King Kalif and Barnabas were sharpening hunting spears toto prepare for their next hunting trip. It had been quite some time since the King and his staff went hunting. Barnabas would hold the end of the spear by the handle while the king sharpened the blade to razor sharpness. They finished the last spear and Barnabas quickly pulled it from the King's grasp. The blade sliced through the King's hand, causing a deep and bloody wound. The King was furious.

"How dare you!" King Kalif shouted. "Now I cannot hunt at my best!"

Barnabas apologized profusely. He thought the king had finished sharpening that spear. He ran to fetch water and a bandage.

"It is for the best," Barnabas whispered while cleaning the king's hand.

"Enough. You are not going on this hunting trip," the King yelled. "I'm banishing you to the cellblock where you will remain until my return. I will deal with you then."

Barnabas obeyed and retreated to the cell block where he was imprisoned.

The next day the king took his staff out for the hunting trip. While pursuing a wild boar, King Kalif was separated from the group. He wandered deep into the woods, eager to capture the large animal. Just as he was closing in, a group of native tribesmen ran in front of him, stopping him in his tracks.

"You come with us," one of them said. Two others grabbed the King by the arms and led him away. They took his spear and brought him to the chief of their tribe.

"Chief, we found the perfect specimen," a Tribesman said.

"Yes, he will do," the Chief replied.

"I will do what?" the King asked nervously. He looked around, confused by what was happening.

"We need to perform a human sacrifice to ensure prosperity over our land," the Chief replied. "We must find one human foreigner who is perfect and pure, kill him, and offer him to the gods."

"You can't kill me, I'm a King!" King Kalif cried.

"All the better for our gift," the Chief said and smiled.

The tribesmen led King Kalif to the sacrificial table. They removed his clothes. Just as they were about to lift him onto the table, one tribesman noticed his hand.

"What is this?" he asked the King.

The tribesman took the bandage off, revealing the king's large, deep dark red cut.

"You will not do. Sacrifice must be free of impurities. You are impure," the tribesman said.

The tribe released him and let him return to his kingdom. The bewildered King returned to his castle and immediately ran to Barnabas.

"You will never guess what happened to me," the King said. He told Barnabas the story.

"It was for the best after all," Barnabas replied coyly.

"Yes, you were right, my old friend. However, how was it the best for you? I threw you in this cell and left you behind."

Barnabas paused thoughtfully.

"If I had gone with you on this hunting trip, the tribesmen would have deemed me pure for the sacrifice and executed me instead of you. By punishing me for my error, you have spared my life," he told the King.

It really was for the best.

Now, I hope you never find yourself on a sacrificial table, but this simple story I tell my son illustrates the fact that disappointment leads to something better. Things happen for a reason. It is natural to be disappointed to begin with but remember that there must be some reason things did not work out. My son's school had a special music program called the Bentley Beats. It was a percussion club made up of about twelve kids. He was really excited to audition to be a part of the group. The time came for his big day, and he went in, banged on the drums with all his heart, and then found out three days later that he did not make the group. It devastated him. It surprised me he did not get selected; he had talent, and I'm not saying that just because he is my son. He plays guitar and violin, so he's musically inclined. He even has an Indian drum kit he likes to play. However, he did not make the cut.

When he came home that day, I told him that maybe it was for the best. "You'll see why in a few weeks," I said. I could not predict the sequence of events that happened next.

A few weeks later, his school had a try-out for their Science Olympiad team. It was kind of like a Scholastic Bowl or Mathletes, but with a scientific flair. On the day of the trial, the Bentley Beats had a mandatory practice. The instructor said all Bentley Beats members could not try out for the Science Olympiad because of the scheduling conflict.

My son went on to this primary competition and made the team! We were so proud of him. Not only did he make the team, but he won first place for his school against other schools in the district. About a week into his new adventure he stopped me in the kitchen and said, "Daddy, you were right. It really was for the best. If I got on to the Bentley Beats, I would not have been able to compete in the Science Olympiad."

I smiled. He got it.

My kids continue to remind me of this lesson. One morning I had an 8:00 a.m. meeting at my corporate office in Houston. When I am home with my family, I like to take my kids to school.

It allows me to spend more time with them.

This particular morning, my daughter was indecisive. First, she could not decide what she wanted for breakfast. Then she did not know how she wanted her hair for the day. Finally, she had a tough time picking out her shoes. Mind you, she is only in kindergarten. With her eventual shoe choice confirmed, we grabbed her brother and set out to school. Unfortunately, we missed our sweet spot to avoid other school commuters and got stuck in traffic.

"It's for the best, Daddy," my son said to me as I sat in the driver's seat, brow furrowed. But after he said that I had to smile. That morning was filled with precious moments that still make me smile today.

When we accept this as fact and know our disappointments will give way to greater things, we become less anxious. We feel less insecure. We're able to curb the root cause of our negative behaviors, which manifest from anxiety and insecurity.

It Is All in Your Head

Our mind is a powerful tool that controls our thoughts, which can ultimately control our destiny. Professor Richard Wiseman of the University of Hertfordshire completed a study on why some people get all the luck while others never get the breaks, they feel they deserve.

Wiseman wanted to know why some people are just plain lucky or unlucky. He placed advertisements in the national newspaper asking for people who felt consistently lucky or unlucky to contact him. "Over the years, 400 extraordinary men and women have volunteered to participate in my research; the youngest eighteen, a student, the oldest eighty-four, a retired accountant. It drew people from all walks of life—businessmen, factory workers, teachers, housewives, doctors, secretaries and salespeople." [21]

Wiseman conducted a simple experiment. He gave the self-identified lucky and unlucky people a newspaper and asked them to look through it. He wanted them to report back how many photographs were inside. Halfway through the paper, he placed a half-page ad that said, "[T]ell the experimenter you have seen this and win $250."

What he found was the "unlucky" people had trouble spotting the ad, and the lucky people found it and turned it in to claim the prize. He determined the anxiety and self-doubt the unlucky people have really distracts them and prevents them from noticing the unexpected. In contrast, the lucky people are at peace, are calm, and are more open to unexpected delights. This is all because of how each person perceives themselves and the world around them. Look how powerful our thoughts are!

"Sometimes you fall down because there is something down there you are supposed to find," (Unknown)

What Does That Have to Do with the Price of Fish?

If we are calm and unafraid of being judged or making mistakes, then we are open to blessings that come as consequences of our mistakes. We won't feel defensive, and we can control our ego. It won't trigger a negative chain of reactions.

Summary

- *We are continuously trying to protect our self-image from imperfection.*

- *Vulnerability is scary, but it is also a superpower.*

- *Mistakes are great teachers.*

---

21 *Richard Wiseman, "The Luck Factor," Skeptical Inquirer 27, no. 3 (May/June 2003), p. 2, https://docplayer. net/9314313-The-power-of-superstition.html.*

Chapter 7: Relinquish Fear of Judgment

I would like to take a moment to talk about the fear of being judged. That is one of the many things that can affect our egos negatively. The fear of being judged stems from what I like to call a self-confidence deficit.

We all have varying degrees of self-confidence. There are many contributing factors that can impact our self-confidence, such as our upbringing, personality preferences, and our surrounding society. However, self-confidence deficits can occur at any stage of our life. We all experience these deficits from time to time.

One occasion, for me, happened in England in 2003. I began my first job in my chosen field at Alaris Medical Systems on September 1. In October, my line manager who hired me left for maternity leave. In the UK, maternity leave can be up to six months. I had just started a new job and my manager left just one month into my post.

My colleagues had developed a strong bond from years of working together. I was an outsider and I felt the effects of being on the periphery of the social circle. I was not motivated to break into the group. I came in each day. I sat down at my desk. I took lunch. I left at the end of my shift. I did not speak to anyone unless it was in a business context. I spent my time alone.

The problem, besides the social isolation, encountered was that no one gave me tasks to do routinely. They routinely had not made arrangements when my line manager left for maternity leave. I did not get a new boss or direction how to complete my work. On the rare occasion I would ask my colleagues for tasks, but they were too busy to help me find my way. My introductory training checklist remained incomplete.

Little did I know that my isolation and hermit tendencies were bothering my colleagues. They made multiple reports against me. I had no idea until the director of my company requested to meet with me.

"I heard these complaints about you, Salman," he said. "Stories of you not integrating with this company, not interacting. What is going on?"

"I just keep to myself," I answered.

"I have heard you use the work internet for personal use, you barely speak to your colleagues—I mean, we will have to have a meeting with human resources," he said firmly.

"Okay," I replied. What else could I say?

I left his office and walked back to my desk. Nothing was going was right for me. I feared I would lose my job.

The UK work environment is a lot different from the US. In the UK, it is hard to get fired, but equally hard to get hired. You must commit egregious offenses to even enter the termination process. Apparently, I was doing just that.

I went home that evening, weighed down by a cloud of depression. On the one hand, I didn't really care if I lost my job or not. Some days I would arrive home and not even turn on the lights. But if I lost my job, how would that look on my resume?

Would I be able to find another job to pay my bills? I had already experienced enough setbacks; I was not ready to face another one.

Usually when faced with adversities, my go-to is God. My faith was a way to get me out of a headspace that weighed me down. I don't go to the mosque often, but I do for holidays, funerals, Eid prayers, and when I needed to clear my head. That evening I walked into my local mosque. When I arrived, the priest, known as a Maulana, was telling everyone a story about a young boy and his uncle. It was a story I had heard many times before.

Qasim ibn al-Hasan was 13 years old. The night before the Battle of Karbala, he asked his uncle Imam Hussein, "Uncle, are we not on the right path?" Qasim was curious, understanding death could be the consequence of their travels. The battle was one against a tyrant ruler. It was a battle for righteousness and freedom.

His uncle Hussein responded, "Of course we are on the right path."

Qasim replied, "If we are on the right path, why should we fear death?" If you are on the right path, consequences do not matter. "It is said," Qasim replied, "For me, death is sweeter than honey." He did not fear the unknown. He did not worry about the future. He did nothing wrong. He was on the right path. Therefore, there was no need to be concerned with consequence. This was brave and noble. When we genuinely believe in something, and stick with it, we gain the courage to proceed. We do not worry about the consequences.

This story really clicked with me that night. I paused for a moment and thought about my brief career with Alaris. "Have I done anything wrong?" After reflecting on that question, I realized

I had not. It was not a crime to be quiet. It was not against company policy to refrain from colleague conversations.

I may have used the internet a few times to look up something of interest, but that too was not an illegal offense. Why worry about the future? If I knew in my heart, I had done nothing wrong, then I truly had nothing to worry about.

I felt something growing inside of me. It was my self-confidence.

The next day I had my meeting with Human Resources. For once, I was not anxious, or worried.

We sat down at a long conference table.

"Salman, you're not pulling your weight around here," the HR representative said. "You don't speak to anyone—you kind of creep out some of your coworkers with your silence and isolation. You are not in a junior position, yet your work ethic reflects such."

She went on, listing a series of grievances they had against me. I sat there patiently, listening, waiting for my turn to speak.

When she finished. I pled my case. "I understand they have perceived me as subpar, but my manager went out on maternity leave in October and no one replaced her," I said. "I have no direct report, no guidance what I, a new employee, should or should not be doing. Everyone here has been with the company for a decent amount of time. They have built friendships. I'm an outsider. Why would I try to infiltrate myself into someone else's established social circle?"

She did not interrupt me.

"I'm not rude or ignorant. I just don't feel I have much in common with my colleagues. They talk about all sorts of inside jokes and things that I just do not understand or have enough knowledge about to contribute to the conversation. I'm new and just trying to make it through each day at this point."

I listed all my attempts to engage in my many tasks. I tried to take initiative, but I did not get enough support from my coworkers.

At the end of my brilliant monologue, she knew they could not fire me. At least not that day. I had made very valid points and shed some light on the cracks of the plan to oust me. She requested I report to my director for the interim until my line manager returned. My probation period lasted six months; they extended it for an additional six months.

I left that meeting buzzing with energy. I wrote all the grievances they mentioned. In fact, I made a list of each one and developed an action plan to address it. This was the most motivation I had felt in a long time. I felt my director and the HR representative made some very valid points and addressed aspects of my work that I could improve upon. I just had to devise a plan to meet their expectations. I needed to learn how to interact with my colleagues. I was determined to make an honest effort.

Even though I did not know my MBTI preferences I realized being quiet and minding my business was not working. I had to find a way within my sphere of interest to engage and interact. I did not do it before because it did not come naturally to me. I stayed in my comfort zone of silence. Since I was in survival mode, I had to do things differently. I did not know analyzing the situation was my strength. But that is what I did. I carefully observed what coworkers were talking about. Girls, booze, dirty politics at work, and soccer (we call it football in the UK) were the hot topics of conversation.

I dove headfirst into my goals. I realized that with my

personality, values, and interests, it's almost impossible for me to engage in these topics, except football. Besides cricket, I really wasn't into any other sports. I researched, read the news, watched old game highlights, and immersed myself with learning everything I could about football. I read the paper every single day to catch up on the latest sport scores, news, football gossip, opinions of ex-players. you name it. I learned everything I could about sports! My colleagues talked about sports a lot.

With my newfound knowledge, I started talking to my colleagues about football, asking them if they had watched the latest games. I attended the weight loss club faithfully for a while. I learned my coworkers' interests. I asked them about their children, pets, and families. I studied the dynamics of my office environment and learned the ins and outs of the social interactions that took place each day.

It was an inspirational and life-changing experience. I learned a whole new culture. I fine-tuned my shortcomings and corrected many of the grievances the HR representative had listed. But it was draining. I never felt like it was fake, but it was a lot of work to be a genuine social butterfly. Especially when I had spent months keeping to myself and living in my own quiet silo.

I would continue to work for Alaris for five years. When I left, I considered everyone around me a friend, and to this day, I still keep in touch with them.

When your weaknesses are brought to light, it is an opportunity to grab the metaphorical microscope and look at them carefully. What can you do to improve upon your weak points? What plan can you make? What action can you take?

Weakness is strengthened by overcoming fear, and it decreases your insecurities. Therefore, lack of confidence is the root of fear.

American writer and poet Suzy Kassem said, "Doubt kills more dreams than failure ever will." [22]

A dangerous weapon that can cripple your self-confidence is aa self-fulfilling prophecy. When you believe a certain element about yourself—typically, a negative belief—you eventually turn that belief into reality.

Say you are a student and all your teachers have labeled you the troublemaker. You start to believe that you are and always will be the troublemaker. You believe your future teachers—who don't know this preconceived identity that was placed on you — will instantly label you the troublemaker. You act more like a troublemaker more because society has convinced you that you are one. That is how dangerous self-fulfilling prophecy is.

I have seen this happen in sports. Take cricket, for example. The South African team is one of the top teams in the world. However, there have been many occasions where the team was labeled as "chokers." Why? In the heat of the match, all the talent and good decision-making seem to dissipate. The team, when under fire, made horrible moves, causing them to blow the game. It is as if the fans, who labeled them as "chokers," have directly affected the way they play the game.

"I believe, therefore I am."

The golden ticket out of this thinking is to recognize it when it is happening and break that cycle of self-fulfilling prophecy.

After graduate school, I took any job I could find in Australia. One of my many jobs was setting up rides and attractions for events. Every weekend I would go to the grounds and help

22 *Suzy Kassem Quotes About Doubt," AZ Quotes, https://www.azquotes.com/author/54644-Suzy_Kassem/tag/ doubt.*

assemble bouncy houses, rides, and tents. I would find the space for each attraction and hammer stakes into the ground to mark each placement.

One day it was brutally hot. I was sweating, and it was Ramadan, so I was fasting until sundown. I was tired, dizzy, and hungry. As I tried to hammer the stake into the ground, it just would not budge. I became angry and frustrated. I took a deep breath and thought, "Did I really spend thousands of dollars and travel halfway around the world to hammer pegs into the ground?"

No, I did not. But I reminded myself to never forget how I felt at that moment as the sweat dripped down my face. I told myself to remember how I felt because I will have better days than this. To this day, whenever I'm struggling, I reach into my memories and dig up those feelings associated with the tougher times in my life. I watch them play out in my head and feel the emotions in my heart.

I tell myself, "I have done this before. I will do it again."

I would not call it a mantra, but I use these words to remind myself of my truth. I find this phrase comforting when I get behind in my work and feel the stress and pressure from my job. I literally repeat the phrase, "I have done this before, I will do it again," 150 times in my head, so it is stuck in my mind for that day.

Finding the right words to inspire you can make a difference. Think about a tough time where you persevered. Try to find a word or phrase that encapsulates how you felt after you overcame a tribulation. You can adopt this as your personal mantra in your darkest moments. Mantras can serve as great shields from the damaging effects of self-fulfilling prophecies.

Doubt and fear can cripple and confuse the mind. Self-confidence brings clarity into the mind and heart.

Summary:

- *The fear of being judged is born out of a self-confidence deficit.*

- *When you believe in something noble, stick with it.*

- *Illuminate and inspect your weakness to turn them into strengths.*

Chapter 8: Unpack Your Self-Deception Box

Now, that we understand that a lack of confidence is rooted in fear, there is another component to it. I would not classify it as a "root," but a contributing factor. That factor is self-deception, which serves as a catalyst to a lack of confidence. As I mentioned before, we think of ourselves as infallible beings. We want to preserve that squeaky-clean image. Self-deception can heighten that desire, thus awakening our fear.

In this chapter, we will discuss self-deception and what happens when we put ourselves in a metaphorical box.

It is easy to fall prey to self-deception. We can be our own worst enemy. Denial fuels self-deception and is a misguided rationalization that occurs within our minds. We are quick to think reality is actuality. Things we see, hear, and sense are real. Therefore, if they are real, that means they are fact. Or does it?

There is a difference between reality and actuality.

I am sure you know someone—including yourself—who has been to the dentist and had to receive laughing gas for a dental procedure. The nitrous oxide takes the patient's mind off the pain and puts them in a state of calm and sometimes makes them giggle.

Meanwhile, the dentist is pulling teeth or drilling holes into an extremely sensitive area filled with nerves. The patient may be laughing. That is a fact. That is the reality. The actuality is that the laughing gas is masking the patient's pain. They are unaware of the pain. Numbed to it. The pain would be there if the gas were not. The cause of the pain is still there.

This example is to illustrate a critical point: what you see might not be the root cause of a situation. The things you witness are 100 percent true, but there may be another layer of elements you are not even aware of.

What You See Is What You Get, Sometimes

A long time ago, I was attending my first auditing training in the UK. The training lasted for five days, and our sessions ran from 8:00 a.m. to 10:00 p.m. It was a residency training for a lead auditor course. We had a very dynamic trainer named Alfred. He had remarkable stories and was charismatic and funny. All the students enjoyed his sessions. He was warm and engaging.

One Thursday night, we noticed someone new sitting in the front of our class. Alfred asked him to introduce himself. He was a journalist, writing an article about the effectiveness of audit training for aa quality and assurance journal. His name was Edward, and he would join us for the evening session.

After introductions, Alfred suggested we take part in a role-play exercise. We had our big auditing test the next morning, and this would be a practical way to study. Alfred would have us write him a nonconformance, and he would defend the actions of his "company," to talk us out of writing it.

They picked a gentleman, a short man in his 50s, for the role-play in front of the class. He began by issuing the nonconformance to Alfred. Alfred immediately jumped to defend his company.

This went on for a few minutes until we saw Alfred getting very frustrated. The student started giving nonsensical reasons he issued the nonconformance. Alfred was not having it. It was 8:00 p.m., we were all exhausted, and the role-play scenario was becoming more and more unrealistic.

"This is not how we do things. This is not right," Alfred said, referring to the role-play.

The student thought he was still in character and continued with his own role-play, offering crazy reasons he was doing it right.

"No, this is how we do things here," the student countered, still missing the cue that Alfred was ending the role-play.

He stayed in character until Alfred suddenly erupted in anger.

"Shut up! Don't you get it?" he shouted.

The class went silent. You could hear a pin drop. I did not even breathe. We didn't think Alfred was capable of such behavior. The student argued back and then, in a huff, went to his desk, picked up his things, and exited the classroom, slamming the door on his way out.

We could tell Alfred felt remorse the second the student left. Nobody knew what to say.

"Let's take a brief break," Alfred said softly, a look of disbelief and regret on his face. He glanced at Edward sitting in the front, furiously scribbling in his notepad. Alfred sighed and wiped his brow. He knew he had made a colossal mistake.

I could not help but wonder what happened to Alfred that night. The next day, he returned to class and was apologetic. Edward, the journalist, reported Alfred for his outburst, saying it was a significant story to write but extremely inappropriate behavior. The company's reputation was at stake. Edward worried

Alfred was unfit for leading these types of trainings, fearing he would decimate any morale trainees had.

Little did Edward (or any of us) know that Alfred was going through a nasty divorce. Despite his personal issue, he still made the time to teach the course when he easily could have canceled to tend to his own life.

Right before our role-playing session, he had received a call from his lawyer with unfavorable results. We were not told what they were, but I assume it might have been about custody or something along those lines. Alfred tried to mask his feelings before the role-play, but the student's inability to recognize the cues Alfred tried to convey really set him off. It brought up his frustrations with his personal life, and out they all came, in front of our entire class.

With this additional information, we understood why Alfred acted the way he did. He could never retract his outburst, but with new understanding, he was, well, forgiven. Alfred was apologetic, especially to the student he embarrassed.

On the "laughing gas" surface, Alfred's behavior has no explanation. Once we learn the deeper root of the pain, we can correlate the outburst to the behavior. Reality and actuality are two vastly different things.

Everyone has a story. Every human is a complex layer of thoughts and emotions, of morals and values. Every individual has a history and a sequence of life events that molded them into the person they are today. Remember Alfred's story when you are interacting with others. Challenge yourself to see beyond the laughing gas and determine what the root cause of others' behavior really is. This will strengthen the superpower known as empathy, which we will talk about later, but it will also help you determine the difference between reality and actuality in everyday situations.

How many times have you heard the story of the mother who always seems angry? She is never happy and is constantly telling off her children. They do not understand what they have done to upset her, but no matter what, she finds something to be upset about.

Turns out, she's upset about something that happened months, if not years! The passive-aggressive behavior manifests in day-to-day interactions. We link the emotions from a past situation to the present day, but we disconnect the behavior. The behavior comes from a place far in the past.

Actuality vs. Reality in the Office

This situation can also play out in the office environment. I once had a supervisor—we will call her Judith—who was brilliant and respected. Overall, she was a delightful woman, until one day she did something that really triggered my ego.

I submitted an audit report recommending a client for certification, and she rejected it, stating the dates on the certificate and the audit cycle were mismatched. Not only did she reject it, but she emailed all the leaders in our company while rejecting my report, thus making me look incompetent to my superiors.

She said it was invalid because of certain requirements and a cycle she was following. Having worked directly with the client, the audit, and the certifications involved, my perspective was correct. I felt she was mixing up regulations, having not been on the ground like my colleagues and me.

It still stung that she felt the need to announce her disagreement with me and my report publicly. Mind you, this entire exchange played out on email. Had she given me the chance to sit down and talk to her, I feel things may have gone differently.

Instead of trying to engage in an email battle of who was right and who was wrong, I tried a new approach. I channeled my empathy and put myself in Judith's shoes. It is never easy tuning into your empathy mode when someone has already triggered your ego.

It was difficult, but I told myself, "There must be something that is bothering her; but what is it?" She was new to this senior level position, and it came with many challenges. Her every move was probably scrutinized, and she wanted to make sure she did not make any mistakes. She needed to assert herself as a leader.

I asked for advice, hoping to steer her in the correct direction. I thanked her for her feedback and told her I needed additional guidance on the matter. I asked for further clarification while weaving my perspective in the text. I was respectful and recognized my position in the hierarchy.

As I engaged in this strategy, I felt a shift in our dynamic. Judith became more open to my argument, and we could work past our disagreement. I knew she would never admit the pressure of the job was causing her to make abrupt decisions, but I understood her perspective and used that to work productively with her.

Let's Talk about Boxes

That leads me into my next lesson: the box. One of my favorite books, The Anatomy of Peace: Resolving the Heart of Conflict by the Arbinger Institute introduced me to the concept of "the box." It all starts with a little dash of self-betrayal. We have the urge to do the right thing or a pleasant thing, but then rationalize our way out of doing it. We betray the urge to do something right.

Enter the box. The box is a place we have set up inside of our minds. It is where we go, and, while "sitting" in the box, we see everything from our perspective. We make ourselves glorified victims and see others as oppressors. We create a defensive model perpetuated by distorted views of the world. It is like we see the world through a giant selfie lens. It is a symbol or a metaphor for how we are interacting with another person.

I remember when my son was only a few months old. At that age, babies cry a lot and they wake up throughout the night for various reasons. One night I tried to get to bed at a decent hour because I had to travel for work at 5:00 a.m. I had a long and hectic day of work ahead of me, and I was a little anxious about it. I felt the stress and pressure of the job along with my newfound responsibilities as a new father.

I laid in bed next to my wife, willing myself to sleep so I would be rested. I finally drifted off to sleep. In the middle of the night, my son woke up crying. My eyes popped open as I lay there. I thought, I should probably get up and hold him and get him to go back to sleep. My heart told me to get up and take care of my son. My mind and my body did something different.

I went into the box. No, I must get up so early. I need my sleep. I must go back to sleep. My wife will take care of him. I'm sure she hears him.

I tried to get back to sleep despite my son's cries echoing from across the room. Mothers are better at comforting their babies. She would do a better job getting him to calm down.

My mind created a litany of reasons I should not have to get up and address my son's distress. I convinced myself to stay in bed. I thought it was my right, as a working father, to stay in bed and sleep when I should have gotten out of bed and given my wife a break. I betrayed myself.

A few minutes passed, and my wife still did not get up. My son continued to cry. Instead of giving in and taking charge, I stayed in the box.

Why is she not getting up? Does she not hear him crying? He needs her.

More time passed and neither of us got out of bed. I was now wide awake, angry and frustrated. It upset me that my wife did not get up and take care of our son; however, in the back of my mind, I knew I was mad at myself.

I betrayed myself with so many justifications and talked myself out of doing the right thing. I was not at peace with myself. I was not at peace with my wife, and I was not at peace with my son, either. Yet I was still in the box and was only seeing my world through my perspective.

After what seemed like forever, my wife got up and tended to our son. I exhausted myself with my inner conflict and fell back asleep. I went to work the next day, agitated and tired. I hung onto fragments of resentment toward my wife. She knew I had to get up early. Why could not she take care of him? Why didn't she help me?

Let's look at her side of the situation. Even though she is a qualified biomaterial scientist, she put aside her career ambitions and became a full-time mother—a noble decision that I admire her for. So, she stayed home to care for our son all day. She cooked, cleaned, and played with him and made sure his needs were met. She was tending to him 24/7, with almost no breaks. My wife ran on limited sleep as she got up to care for my son when he cried in the middle of the night. I did not honor these things.

Why won't you help me? She was probably thinking. I take care of him all day and you are away at work. The least you can do is get up right now so I can get some sleep. It is your turn.

As I lay there, eyes shut, not moving, she was probably thinking, "Can't you take care of him for once in your life?"

How does one get out of the box?

In Anatomy of Peace, there is a simple acronym to remember: NOPE. How great is that? You find yourself in the box, and you remember: NOPE.

THE CHOICE DIAGRAM

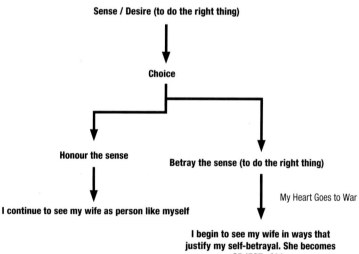

The first step is to notice the indications of being in the box. Notice the red flags. Do you feel angry or judged? Are you blaming the other person? Is there resentment in your heart? Do you feel you deserve better, or are you questioning why the situation is happening to you in the first place?

A good red flag is the word "but." When I was in the box: "I should get up, BUT I have to work tomorrow and get up early and need sleep." The word "but" leads to a world of justification. It is an excellent red flag.

The Better-Than Box

View of Myself	View of Others
Superior	Inferior
Important	Incapable / Irrelevant
Virtuous / Right	False / Wrong
Feelings	**View of the World**
Impatient	Competitive
Disdainful	Troubled
Indifferent	Needs Me

The I-Deserve Box

View of Myself	View of Others
Meritorious	Mistaken
Mistreated / Victim	Mistreating
Unappreciated	Ungrateful
Feelings	**View of the World**
Entitled	Unfair
Deprived	Unjust
Resentful	Owes Me

The Must-Be-Seen-As Box

View of Myself	View of Others
Need to be well	Judgmental
Thought of fake	Threatening
	My audience
Feelings	**View of the World**
Anxious / Afraid	Dangerous
Needy / Stressed	Watching
Overwhelmed	Judging Me

The Worse-Than Box

View of Myself	View of Others
Not as good	Advantaged
Broken / Deficient	Privileged
Fated	Blessed
Feelings	**View of the World**
Helpless	Hard / Difficult
Jealous / Bitter	Against me
Depressed	Ignoring me

Out-of-the-Box Space

Once you have identified your red flags, find an out-of-the-box space. It may help to remove yourself from the physical space — we are talking about a mental space. We need help to see and think differently about the person or people we have "in the box" feelings about.

For example, if someone is burned out by their job, they probably find fault in many of their colleagues. They may see their colleagues or their boss as lazy, inconsiderate, or plain lousy. This individual probably sees themselves as a victim. "I am a hardworking individual who goes above and beyond, but no one will recognize me for it."

Now, put that person in an out-of-box space, try to recall what it was like when you started a brand-new job. The feelings of hope and possibility were in the air. They treated all the colleagues with respect (until you got to know them a little better). This fresh mindset is an out-of-box space. The burnt out individual needs to reframe their thinking, even temporarily, to banish the victim mindset. The person still may think they are hardworking and have a lot to offer, but this time they see opportunity, not detriment.

Another example is this. Let's say I go into the office and my coworker says, "Salman, you're looking fat today." I will take offense to it. It is embarrassing to hear. I will resort to the victim mindset and wonder why my colleague is so bluntly picking on me. But if my daughter says, "Daddy, you look fat today," I laugh. What an odd thing to say. (She actually tells me that several days a week. I suspect I may need to embark on a diet!) My relationship with my daughter differs from my relationship with my colleague. Therefore, if I apply the right mindset to the comment, it no longer bothers me. I am in an out-of-box space.

The biggest takeaway is that "if we want to invite others to change, we need to offer out-of-the-box space to them, which requires we be out of the box toward them ourselves." [23]

Think about people you have an out-of-box relationship with. Notice the characteristics of that relationship. Things are different, right? That is your goal. This is the out-of-box space you are striving for. You can also drum up memories of places, events, and things that are positive and provide great feelings for you. By dwelling on the positive emotions that come up, you can slowly transport yourself to an out-of-box space, which will allow you to move onto the next step.

Ponder the Situation Anew

Next, we must ponder the situation anew. Our ego has calmed down. Picture the ego taking an enormous sigh and letting all the triggers melt away. It distracts our mind with the wonderful feelings from our out-of-box space. Our heart is calm, and we feel at peace. Now it is time to investigate the relationship that put you in the box. With a fresh perspective, we can now look at both sides of the relationship and determine what needs to be done.

Imagine you're climbing a mountain. You are feeling exhausted as you make your way to the top. Negative feelings swirl in your head. "Why am I doing this? What is the point? I'm so tired, and I want to quit." As you ascend the mountain, you continue to envelope yourself in these feelings.

Until you reach the top and take in the spectacular view. Everything feels worth it at that moment. The view is breathtaking. It fills you with accomplishment and positivity. Going back down

---

23 *The Arbinger Institute, The Anatomy of Peace, 254.*

the mountain does not seem that bad because you'll be thinking about those memories from the top that made you feel good.

The next time you climb a mountain, you can remember how it felt to be on the top. This is exactly what is going out of the box and pondering your situation anew looks like. With that extra vantage point, we can now execute the actions we're seeing as per our adjusted view.

Execute What You Learned

When I look back at the situation with my wife, that night I refused to get up and take care of my crying son, I see things differently. I'm so far removed from the moment; I don't bear resentment or entitlement. I can see my wife's perspective as clear as Caribbean waters. I recognize her feelings and my self-betrayal. This self-awareness of the box allows me to ponder many situations anew.

I may never forgive myself for my past self-betrayals, but now I am determined not to repeat my mistakes. I am not infallible. I still make mistakes, but every time I make one, I feel the pain of self-betrayal and find myself even more determined not to repeat it. I may have reduced the frequency of those mistakes, but I am still human and imperfect. Like all humans, I have plenty of room for improvement.

Learning to get out of the box will take time. It is important to remind ourselves that we will always face moments of self-betrayal, denial, and justification. Those feelings we feel will never go away. That is important because if we felt nothing, we would not be human! However, this knowledge of the box can help us recognize when we are in it, and when others are in it.

With practice we can master removing ourselves from the box and gravitating to a peaceful heart and open mind.

Summary

- *Observation and actuality can differ because of elements and situational layers you cannot see.*
- *The box is a place we have set up inside of our minds, where we see everything from our own perspective.*
- *To get out of the box, remember NOPE: Notice; find an Out-of-the-box space; Ponder the situation anew; and Executed what you learned.*

Chapter 9: Asking the Right Questions, Listening the Right Way

We now have a greater understanding of personality types, the ego, ego triggers, actuality, and reality. I hope you have learned a lot about yourself in these past few chapters. I am still learning a lot about myself today. As I have said before, self-awareness is essential in any relationship. The next focus is awareness of others. We had a peek at it in Chapter Three when we looked at the unique MBTI types. Now it is time to learn ways we can grow in our awareness of others.

In this chapter we will discuss awareness, how to ask the right questions, and the importance of active listening.

Awareness of others comes down to several tactics. One of these is how we ask questions. It sounds simple, but it can be complex. For us to gather information about the other person or group, we must ask questions in a manner that does not trigger the ego. Once the ego is triggered, it takes a lot of work to calm it. This is how we build rapport.

What I learned from my elders and gurus is that in business interactions, the best way to build rapport is to start with an informal conversation. We see this play out many times in our lives. I think a favorite topic might be the weather! However, let's not focus on the weather as our gateway to rapport-building. We want to gain information about the other person, and the weather will not help us in this endeavor.

Start by noticing something about the individual. Can you recall from Chapter Three my experience with Abby and Charles, my very introverted colleague and client? I was standing in the kitchen fixing myself a cup of coffee when Charles walked in. He reached into the cabinet and pulled out a coffee mug with a Sheffield United logo on the side. I used this bit of information to start an informal conversation with him about his favorite soccer team. That conversation led into another conversation about our wives and children. By the conclusion of the exchange, I had established rapport and put us both on an equal and human playing field.

It was during this exchange where I also engaged in active listening, a special way of responding to the person speaking to you, assuring them you are listening and understand. Have you ever had a conversation with someone who kept replying with "yeah" and "uh-huh"? That is not actively listening.

An active listener maintains eye contact, rarely interrupts, and asks questions only to increase understanding. When Charles said he had season tickets to the games and took his family from time to time, that was an invitation for me to ask about his family and gain more information. I did not interrupt his side of the conversation until a clear pause presented itself. Then I interjected with a little information about my family to lay a foundation of common ground.

When you practice active listening, you listen with your eyes, your ears, and your heart. You look at the other person and observe and process their body language. You listen to what they are saying, instead of waiting for a break to interject with your own side of the story. And you listen with your heart. A genuine active listener is attuned to the conversation and makes the exchange meaningful for both parties. By listening with your heart, you defer and bury all judgments you may have about the other person or the context of the conversation.

To remember these tips, there is a handy listening mnemonic: LISTEN. It stands for Look interested; Incisive question at the right time; Silence is golden; Test your understanding through paraphrasing; Encourage through non-verbal cues; and Neutralize your feelings.

The Right Questions

If active listening is the groundwork for a fruitful exchange, our questions are our building blocks. Choosing the right questions is paramount. One wrong question, and you can throw off your entire exchange. You can turn a peaceful person into a defensive person.

Picture a pyramid. On the very top, you find the most effective questions. At the bottom are the least effective types of questions. Let's start at the bottom first. The least effective types of questions you can ask another person are "yes/no" questions. These questions demand little of the responder. They are close-ended and can steer a conversation to a grinding halt. You cannot extract much information out of these types of questions.

Slightly more effective but still resting at the bottom of the pyramid are "where" questions. These are specific and can often elicit a brief response. Unless you are looking for a specific and concise response, there are better questions you can answer.

Let's say we asked someone, "Where are you from?" In that context, "where" makes sense. However, "Where did you put that document?" could not only appear accusatory but will also not lead to much information-gathering in an initial exchange. Remember that we're talking about new exchanges or situations where you need to establish common ground to have a productive and peaceful interchange.

Not that you can never ask someone a "where" question. This is merely to illustrate that "where" is not as effective as other questions.

"Who" and "when" questions are above "where" in the question pyramid. These are good middle-level questions. Above that is "What?" "What?" is an excellent question that can illicit many descriptive responses. "What?" is a gateway into greater explanations beyond your opening inquiry.

But the mother of all questions, the most effective question in information-gathering and establishing rapport, is "how?" "How" questions sit on the very top of the pyramid. Often in my audits, instead of asking, "What did you do?" I will say, "How did you do this?" "How?" is an inviting question. It assumes you do not know something but want to know more. It can elevate the other party during conversation. There is a praise to it. That makes it effective.

Considering the above question types, which one is missing?

"Why?"

If I could give each one of you red flags to wave and flares to ignite to encourage you to avoid asking a "why" question, I would. "Why" is the worst type of question you can ask someone. The question itself projects a need for clarification, justification, and explanation.

"Why did you do that?" Perpetuates a sense that something is wrong. Have you ever had a supervisor call you into her office and say, "Why did this happen?" The intention is not always to assume the other person is at fault, but the perception is there. Knowingly, but more often subconsciously, egos are triggered by "why" questions.

To illustrate this further, let's look at questions in order from least powerful to most powerful:

Are you satisfied with your job?

When have you been most satisfied in your job?

How do you feel the most satisfied in your job?

Avoid: Why are you satisfied with your job? That assumes they are satisfied, and maybe they are not!

Questions should always show curiosity.

Empathy

Now that we have practiced active listening and asked engaging questions, it is time to listen to our hearts. A fundamental element that strengthens interactions, and builds trust is empathy.

Empathy is the ability to understand and share in the feelings of others. Active listening helps us hear and understand what the other person is feeling. We can absorb that emotion and really put ourselves in the other person's shoes. Why do they feel sad today? What excites them? If I were in the same situation, would I be angry? Empathy comes from an innate need for human connection; however, it must be genuine.

Have you ever been in a situation when someone tells you, "Yeah, I know how you feel." How did that statement make you feel? Was the other person trying to show empathy? This response is better than ignoring or rejecting a person altogether, but there are much better ways to communicate empathy genuinely. We must be mindful to not appear patronizing or condescending.

The other person is coming from a selfish angle. They think that by saying, "I know exactly how you feel," you will feel comfort and camaraderie. Unfortunately, all that person did was make your interchange about themselves.

Instead of being quick to respond with "I have been there," really listen to what the person is saying and try to comprehend the emotions around their story. Then, if you are sure you know how they feel, find a comparable situation in your own life, and offer the story if it's appropriate. Know your audience. Some people just want validation of their feelings.

You can channel the empathy in others to defuse or improve an interaction. I have mentioned this before, but when I'm completing an audit and I must issue a nonconformance, my client is usually not happy about it. If they become despondent, I let them know that it is not that bad.

I try to share with them all the benefits they will see once they take corrective action and receive certification. If my client is still upset, I hold up a metaphorical mirror. I tell them that if I do not write the nonconformance, I might lose my job. I ask them, gently, if they want that to happen. They almost always respond with a quick "no."

By using this tactic, I have helped them channel their own empathy—their empathy for me! It is helpful because this diffuses the situation, and the client accepts the result. They still might not be happy about it, but they accept the nonconformance.

I also share instances when I received a nonconformance and how I felt. I tell my clients stories of my embarrassment, frustration, and anger. I let them know how embarrassed I was. We often see nonconformance as a sign of incompetence, and any reference to that is an ego trigger. By sharing these stories, I lay equal ground and allow my clients to see the empathy within me.

When empathy comes from a genuine place, beautiful and honest things unfold.

Body Language

We have talked a lot about verbal cues, from actively listening to the right questions. Let's explore nonverbal communication. Body language is just as important as asking the right questions.

Remember when I was at my sister-in-law's party looking angry and agitated? I did not know my face was portraying my emotions for the world to see. I was anxious about my upcoming workweek, but to those around me, I looked dissatisfied with the present environment. Body language and voice depend on what we are thinking and feeling each moment.

From an early age, we learn to pick up and interpret the body language of others. As we grow older, we find many opportunities to fine-tune this skill. When we were young children, we knew when our parents were upset or stressed. They did not have to tell us they were worried, we could tell by their furrowed brow, distracted nature, and hunched shoulders, among other indicators.

As adults, whether we realize it, we analyze others' body language from the second they come into our view. We notice if people exude confidence with tall posture and straight shoulders. We look at people's faces to decipher their authentic emotions. We note how people walk, how people present themselves, and how people react to the world around them.

When you enter a space, keep your breathing low and calm in your body. By emulating a calming presence, you will evoke a calm presence in the other person or party. You can set the tone of the room by controlling your thoughts, feelings, and body language.

While in conversation with another person, it is important to mirror their body language to keep the interaction on neutral ground. This will establish a nonverbal rapport. The first thing is to establish the same physical level —make sure there is not a palpable height differentiation. If one person is standing and the other is sitting, it establishes a power dynamic.

Eye level should be just that: level and equal. Match the other's posture closely, but not exactly. You do not want the other person to think you are mimicking them. Observe the tone of their body. Is it relaxed? Is it anxious? What tone do you hope to establish in the conversation? Set the physical playing field to an equal level and emulate that tone. If you are at ease, they will eventually feel at ease. If they are angry, you don't want your body to be angry too. That will perpetuate the negative emotion.

A single misread glance can trigger Egos. We must realize that whatever is on our mind is also on our face.

There was a time when I did not follow any of these guidelines. Back in 2009, I was still relatively new as an auditor in Derbyshire, England. Our company would take over a certification from one of our competitors.

While on-site at a company formerly audited by our competitor, I noticed something that startled me. There were three of us standing in a sizeable meeting room surrounded by medical devices. I looked at the products and immediately realized the company was selling medical devices without the proper regulatory approvals. They had products on display in a meeting area that did not have the right certification stickers (CE mark). I glanced at each one and saw they were all lacking the proper mark.

I was new to the field, and when you are new, you spot discrepancies quickly. Its literally your job to spot abnormalities.

So, I interrupted the conversation.

"Excuse me, but why do these devices lack a CE mark? This is wrong," I said bluntly.

"This is illegal," I continued.

"No, it is not," a woman quickly replied.

"Yes, it is," I countered. "These devices need the proper certification marks to be in compliance."

I know I looked horrified. I felt horrified and incredulous.

"These devices are properly licensed," the woman said, her voice slightly elevated.

"I believe you are mistaken. This is illegal, and there are all sorts of penalties," I said firmly. I could not believe this was happening.

The CEO and quality manager left the meeting. I stood there defiantly, looking at the devices.

Suddenly the quality manager came back in.

"My boss wants you to leave immediately," she said, her face red with embarrassment.

It dumbfounded me. I opened my mouth to contest, but nothing came out. I was only doing my job! I had never been removed from the premises before. I never thought in my wildest dreams something like this would happen.

Unbeknownst to me, I offended the head of the company. I must have embarrassed the entire team with my questions, my antics, my body language, and the way I approached the situation.

When I arrived at the meeting room before this transpired, the few people in the room were sitting and I was standing, thus changing the dynamics of the brief conversation. I asked the wrong questions. My body language was threatening. I made them feel inferior.

I did not know I did that! I did not mean to. I just wanted to make sure everything was compliant before we moved forward. I thought I was doing my job. My intention was not the consequence. However, they felt that way. Their feelings were 100 percent true.

I walked out of the building stunned and humbled. I did not want to tell my wife why I was home early. I didn't want to tell my boss what had just happened. I had never been so embarrassed. My boss eventually had to deal with a report the company made against me.

I felt a bit vindicated when I found out they were not in compliance. They needed to comply, just as I thought. It triggered their egos. However, the way I approached the entire scenario was wrong. There were measures I should have taken that would have led to a more favorable result, for both parties.

Now when I conduct audits, I tell every client they have a right to kick me out if they feel it is necessary. Most of them laugh and ask why they would ever do such a thing. I just smile and say, "It is your right."

I have now presented two vastly different situations in this book. The first takes us back to chapter 1, when we talked about the infamous Colton Barns. Imagine if I lacked self-awareness for that venture! From his obvious disdain for minorities, to his lack of knowledge regarding Brexit, Colton provided many opportunities for me to become provoked.

What if I was aggressive or my body language was inappropriate? Might he have pulled his gun on me? But I was mindful and aware. I used my principles and lessons learned over the years and got out of that situation with a shake of the hand and an emotional tear falling from my client's eye.

However, in 2009, I did everything wrong. I asked the wrong questions, used the wrong body language, did not practice a drop of empathy. I thought I was right and took great measure to convey that to the client. Those people were gracious! They did not have guns and never threatened me, but I still behaved in a deplorable and unaware manner. In 2009 I was unaware, confident, and ignorant. In 2016 I was aware, confident, and mindful. What a difference seven years can make!

Summary:

- *When asking a question, choose "how?" instead of "why?"*
- *Active listening means listening with the entire body, making eye contact, and being in the present moment.*
- *Empathy is to place ourselves in another's shoes, feeling their feelings while being authentic.*

Chapter 10: The Four Quadrants of Emotional Intelligence

Throughout our lives we build more awareness about the world and the people in it. In Chapter Four, I mentioned I had three tools I rely on to inform my awareness of others. Now it is time to discuss the third tool: emotional intelligence.

In this chapter, we will explore the concept of emotional intelligence through the lens of the Four Quadrants of Emotional Intelligence. [24]

Emotional intelligence is the ability to recognize emotions. It is the ability to differentiate between different feelings and label them appropriately. Emotional intelligence allows us to use this emotional information to guide thinking and behavior. Let's unpack that.

So far, we have talked about the different aspects of this definition, but now it is time to inspect it further using different lens. The Four Quadrants of Emotional Intelligence is an excellent place to start.

Self-Awareness/Intensity

Let's understand self-awareness with a slightly different perspective. Let's call it "intensity." Once we understand the

---

24 *"What Is Emotional Intelligence? Why Should I Care?", Jane Ryan & Associates, LLC, November 15, 2016, https://www.janeryanassociates.com/apps/blog/show/44008904-what-is-emotional-intelligence-and-why-should-i-care.*

Daniel Goleman's
Model

	Recognition	Regulation
Personal Competence	**Self-Awareness** • Self-confidence • Awareness of your emotional stage • Recognizing how your behavior impacts others • Paying attention to how others influence your emotional state.	**Self-Management** • Getting along well with others • Handling conflict effectively • Clearly expressing ideas and information • Using sensitivity to another person's feelings (empathy) to manage interaction successfully.
Social Competence	**Social Awareness** • Picking up on the mood in the room • Caring what others are going through • Hearing what the other person is 'really' saying.	**Relationship Management** • Getting along well with others • Handling conflict effectively • Clearly expressing ideas/information • Using sensitivity to another person's feelings (empathy) to manage interactions successfully.

concept of intensity in this context, it will be a lot easier to link back to "self-awareness." Feelings can be labeled by degrees of intensity. What if you walked into a meeting room and put down your bag in your chosen seat? Knowing it would be a long meeting, you walked out to use the restroom. When you returned, you noticed someone moved your bag to a different seat, much further away from the one you chose.

Ask yourself, "What am I feeling in this moment?" Are you irritated (low intensity)? What about frustrated (medium intensity)? Depending on how your day is going, you might even feel outraged (high intensity). Another way of looking at it is: do I just feel angry, or do I feel like I want to punch someone? The actions that hypothetically accompany your feelings can clue you in to their intensity.

Let's say you had a long day at work. When you arrive at your home, you open the door and all your friends are there. They are throwing you a surprise birthday party! You feel happy. Are you feeling glad (low intensity)? What about cheerful (medium intensity)? If you really love surprise parties, you might feel exuberant (high intensity).

Let's look at the hypothetical actions. Are you just smiling? Do you want to hug everyone in the room? Do you want to run into the crowd of friends and high-five them and jump around?

This self-awareness is built upon the ability to recognize your own emotions and intensity they carry. This creates a greater understanding of yourself and your situation, which will soon apply to others.

Self-Management

After the self-awareness quadrant is the self-management quadrant. This is an action square. Now that we have identified how we're feeling and to what degree, what do we do about it? It is important to note that all feelings are okay. We can feel whatever we want. However, not all behaviors are okay. So, we can feel like we are so angry we could punch someone in the face, but it is not appropriate to punch someone in the face.

The self-management quadrant invites us to explore what we

want to feel, at and what we need to do to feel that way. So, if we are sad, how do we want to feel? Happy? Calm? Relaxed? Once we identify the feeling we want to feel, we can then decide what steps to take to get there.

So, knowledge of the emotional intensity scale is important. If someone is feeling, depressed, thinking happy thoughts or looking at happy pictures will not help them overcome that depression. If someone is just feeling a little glum, these tactics might just work.

Remember my story about my supervisor, Judith, who emailed all of leadership to point out an error she believed I made? When I saw that email, it outraged me. It triggered my ego, and I could not believe she would put me on an email blast like that. I had a pocket full of choice words for her. I wanted her to know how wrong she was and how ignorant it was of her to email everyone.

First, I checked-in with how I was feeling. I had a high-intensity degree of emotion: seething. I wanted to get to a low-intensity emotion, such as annoyed, and then eventually switch to calm. What did I need to do to get to that point?

The next thing I did was draft an email of what I wanted to say in my high-intensity state. It was bloody awful. I got all my aggressions out but did not send it. Instead, I sent it the next morning. When my anger and steam had dissipated a little, I realized this action would not get me the results I wanted. I changed my original email by first taking out all the harsh words. Eventually, by the time I was finished editing, it was a new email, in a courteous and respectful tone.

I expressed myself eloquently, drawing attention to the points I believed Judith and I disagreed upon. I did not mention the inciting incident: her sending the corporate-wide email. Instead, I focused on the issue at hand: our disagreement on procedure.

I had a few back-and-forth emails with Judith, and all of them were neutral and respectful. I finally got somewhere and opened a dialogue with her about the discrepancies that kept occurring with this auditing case.

If I remained at a high-intensity emotion and sent my seething email, she could have fired me. If I reduced my action to a medium-intensity-emotion email, I would not have been fired but I would have been seen as outrageously defensive. Remember: I wanted to get to a place where I felt less angry and calmer. The only way to do that was to check in with my emotions, identify their root cause, and determine the best course of action to reach my desired result.

Social Awareness

However, emotional intelligence is not just about looking at the self; it is also about recognizing and correctly identifying emotions in others. The third quadrant is an "others"-facing quadrant. It is social awareness.

Social awareness takes what we learned in the first quadrant and applies that knowledge with an exterior focus. We look at others and ask ourselves, "What is that person feeling, and how did those feelings arise?" Notice we don't not ask ourselves WHY they feel the way they do. Instead, we open the gates of exploration with a HOW question. How did the feelings happen?

We do this because it helps create a sense of understanding for the other person's emotions. If we ask why they are feeling a certain way, we may never know the answer. We are not them. We are not walking in their shoes. We don't have the same brain or heart or nerves. But if we change the lens to ask ourselves how the feelings happened, it becomes easier to surmise the inciting action or circumstance.

Remember when my infant son was crying in the middle of the night and I was in the box, refusing to get up to care for him? My wife was furious with me. What if I asked myself, "Why does she feel angry?" If I asked myself that question, I could easily stay in the box. "Why?" can trigger defensive feelings and thought patterns. Instead, I would ask myself, "How did my wife's feelings happen?" They happened after I didn't get up to care for our son, who was crying because I wanted to sleep. Asking "Why?" promotes reasoning. Asking "How?" promotes tangible evidence.

Another example of social awareness is what happened to Alfred during that auditor training many years ago. Alfred's outburst with the role-playing student had nothing to do with the role-play at hand. In fact, it was a reaction to something happening in Alfred's personal life. If we ask "why" Alfred's outburst happened, we could surmise that the student's lack of awareness agitated him. Alfred tried to tell him that his role-playing was ineffective, but the student thought they were still in the role-play, not receiving real-time feedback on their performance.

If we ask "how" Alfred's outburst happened, we can trace the behavior and the emotions to the call he received before leading the training session. We understand that Alfred was not in the best state of mind that day. He was upset because of a personal circumstance but felt it was his duty to carry on and teach the class. As the student in the role-play continued to act as if he did not understand or hear Alfred's direction, Alfred felt more and more unheard. His emotions escalated to the highest degree.

Social awareness awakens our sense of empathy. By continually improving this skill, we can channel our empathy for others.

Relationship Management

The last quadrant is the relationship management square. This too relates to awareness of others. Remember, we cannot determine how another person may want to feel. If someone is sad, we cannot just assume they want to feel happy. In this square, we ask ourselves, "How do I want the other person to feel?" and "What do I need to do to make them to feel that way?"

When someone is angry at us, we want them to feel not angry with us. Using self-awareness, we can determine what actions we need to take to help the other person not feel angry with us. These questions and self-reflection may seem complicated, but you are probably already doing many of these things without even thinking about it.

When you introduce a new person into your friend group, you probably go the extra mile to make them feel welcome. When you see someone who is uncomfortable, instinct tells you to help them feel more comfortable.

Remember: what we may want someone to feel may change as we gain more information and insight on them. I think that student in our auditing class wanted Alfred to feel ashamed because he felt ashamed. After learning the root cause of Alfred's outburst, perhaps that feeling changed. Maybe that student wanted Alfred to feel peace or acceptance.

Putting It All Together

Let's sum everything up using the bag example. You walked into the meeting room, put your bag at your seat, and walked out, only to return and find someone moved your bag. The first step is to check in with yourself. How do you feel, and to what degree do you feel that emotion? Next, how do you want to feel? Do you want to feel calm? Do you want to feel happy? What do you need to do to feel happy? Do you need to ask who moved your bag and get an understanding of why the action occurred? Start there.

Perhaps someone moved your bag because they forgot their glasses and wanted to sit in your seat so they could see better. Maybe without realizing it, you put your bag in a reserved seat and someone moved it so you would not get in trouble.

Let's say someone moved your bag because they did not want to sit next to you. Have your feelings changed? Maybe you have moved from angry to defensive. Do you ask why, or do you just take your new seat and develop a plan on how to address the situation later?

The Four Quadrants of Emotional Intelligence is an excellent tool to explore further in our own personal lives. There are also many things we can do to practice the concepts in each quadrant.

For self-awareness, one of the most important things we can do is stop treating our emotions as positive or negative feelings. We label feelings such as angry, shame, and fear as negative. We label feelings such as happy, excited, and proud as positive. We Instead of labeling our feelings as positive or negative, just acknowledge that those feelings exist. Remember, all feelings are okay.

But not all behaviors are okay. If you were so angry that someone moved your bag, and you threw it at the other person, that would not be okay. However, if you feel outraged, that is fine! You feel what you feel, and that is 100 percent acceptable. What you do with those feelings is what is important.

Another strategy we can implement is to know who and what pushes our buttons. Everyone has their own set of unique triggers. Awareness of these triggers is essential for diffusing them.

Consider making a list of things that annoy and upset you. Do you see any patterns or trends? This is a great first step in identifying your triggers so you can acknowledge them or avoid them.

Self-Management Strategies

Two strategies of self-management include creating an emotion vs. reason list and visualize yourself succeeding. If we write a list of feelings we typically feel and then next to that list, write a few things that typically make us feel that way, we can uncover some patterns of behavior and emotions that run prevalent in our lives. The more we know about ourselves, the greater our self-awareness (and other-awareness as well).

What about strategies for social awareness? Some things we can try are watching body language, practicing the art of listening, and people-watching. Relationship management strategies include avoiding giving mixed signals, taking feedback well, and complementing the person's emotions or situation. By reading their emotional thermometer, we can adjust to balance the emotion or situation at hand.

Do you remember when I was driving, and the police officer was driving slowly in the passing lane while talking on his phone? (page 94). I passed him abruptly, and he pulled me over. Remember how he shouted and screamed at me? Instead of reacting to the emotions I was receiving, I tried to balance the situation.

I calmly and politely apologized over and over, like a broken record. After a few minutes, I could bring him down from a screaming tone to a conversational tone. In the end, he did not write me a ticket. I believe that is because he was on his phone and he should have been. Also, I do not believe he had evidence of me speeding because I wasn't. However, by analyzing the situation, I could balance out the emotions and bring the emotional atmosphere back down to a normal level.

That was a notable example of using self-management and relationship management. I took inventory of my own emotions. I took inventory of the police officer's emotions. How did his feelings happen? He felt I was rude and arrogant when I sped past him. He felt I broke the law (although I didn't). He was angry. He was shouting. I wanted him to stop shouting. To get him to a point where he was less angry, I apologized and mirrored the behavior I wanted to see from him. I left without a ticket (or getting arrested), and he left with a little less anger in his heart. It was a win-win!

I am still trying to master these skills. It takes time and practice. Emotional intelligence is no silver bullet. Honestly, it takes a lifetime of practice to master self-awareness and awareness of others. These skills are worth practicing! They can help us improve our relationships and interactions with everyone around us.

Summary:

- *Emotional intelligence is the capacity to recognize your own and other people's emotions, to differentiate between feelings and label them appropriately, and to use emotional information to guide thinking and behavior.*
- *The Four Quadrants of Emotional Intelligence are:*
  - *intensity*
  - *self-management*
  - *social awareness*
  - *relationship management*
- *Self-management strategies include creating an emotion vs. reason for emotion list, visualization, and journaling.*

Chapter 11: Exploring the Political Skills Model

Now that we have introduced the Four Quadrants of Emotional Intelligence, let's dive into another group of quadrants. These quadrants are about behaviors. When building our awareness of others, the Baddeley and James political skills model [25] is a brilliant tool for identifying behaviors related to integrity and political awareness.

First, it is important to note that when we say "political," we mean nothing negative. Often, when we hear "office politics" or "being political," a negative connotation is attached. Politics are okay to mention and are normal to talk about. Politics are about interacting with and knowing things about people. It is up to us how we use the word. For this chapter and through most of this book, political means relational.

Political Skills Model [26]

The tool is broken into four quadrants. The x-axis represents levels of integrity. The low end of the spectrum represents those who manipulate and may use others for their own advantage. The high end is for those who act with high integrity. What do we mean by integrity? Integrity is being honest and having strong

25 The Political Animals at Large," *Alchemy Performance Assistant, https://www.alchemyformanagers.co.uk/topics/thExUEu55GwBEw4D.html*
26 Simon Baddeley and Kim James, *"Owl, Fox, Donkey or Sheep: Political Skills for Managers," Management Learning 18, no. 1 (April 1987), 3–19.*

moral principles, a true-north moral compass. Those with high integrity are other-serving instead of self-serving. People with high integrity look out for everyone else's interests, not just their own.

Let's consider the y-axis. It represents a level of awareness of things. By "things" we mean environmental factors, the emotions of others and even the motivation of others. Someone with a low political awareness might not pick up on social cues. Imagine you are having a conversation with three people. After about ten minutes, you need to leave to go to an appointment. At first you drop hints into the conversation, stating you must leave soon. However, one person keeps going on and on about a topic, barely coming up for air and ignoring your subtle hints. This person may lack political awareness. They might not be accustomed to detecting subtle (and sometimes blatant) social cues.

The culmination of the measurements within the Baddeley and James tool categorizes behaviors into four animal groups: sheep, donkey, fox, and owl. As we traverse through life and navigate the complicated scope of relationships both in our personal and professional lives, we move through the quadrants.

Remember: they categorize behaviors, not personalities. We exhibit a myriad of behaviors during our lifetime. It is rare for someone to remain in the same quadrant throughout their adult life. As humans, we are capable of all these behaviors.

Sheep

In this model, we classify individuals who have high integrity but low political awareness as sheep. Sheep rely on authority. In a work situation, they are given lots of work. Sheep stick to the organizational rules without questioning them. They have a deep sense of loyalty to superiors. They are hard workers who are frequently taken advantage of. They believe a reward sits at the end of their labors, but the road to that reward continues to get longer and longer. Sheep are blind to hidden messages and innuendos. They do not read between the lines because they see what is written as the lines. They are wonderful people, and they are often innocent to a fault.

A common misconception is that sheep are simple and sometimes dumb. This is not true. Sheep are not dumb, but they may become fixated on a task without realizing the outcome. In an office setting, someone may give a sheep a report to comb through and look for errors.

Sheep want to do the right thing, so they comb through the report and look for errors. However, they may have been given that task to bring someone else down. The sheep finds errors in the report and gives it back to their supervisor or whoever delegated the task to them. Now, whoever wrote the report is in trouble for all the errors. The sheep would not recognize a devious plot if it fell and hit them on the nose.

A great example of sheep behavior is President Garrett Walker (Michel Gil) from the Netflix series *House of Cards*. President Walker has the skills of a good president. He is normal and relatable. What he does not realize is that Frank Underwood (Kevin Spacey) is quietly undermining his relationship with his vice president, Jim Matthews (Dan Ziskie). Frank eventually convinces Jim that his job as vice president is a mediocre and powerless one. Jim goes off to run for another turn as governor of Pennsylvania, leaving Walker vice president-less. Of course, he nominates Frank Underwood (his plan all along). Of course, Frank manages to weasel his way into the Oval Office and basically blackmail Walker to the point of resigning.

What makes Walker a sheep is not only that he fell for all of Frank Underwood's carefully laid traps (more on Underwood later), but also that he still sort of liked Frank. Walker was grateful for the presidential pardon he received for all of the scandalous stuff he did. Sheep are very gullible.

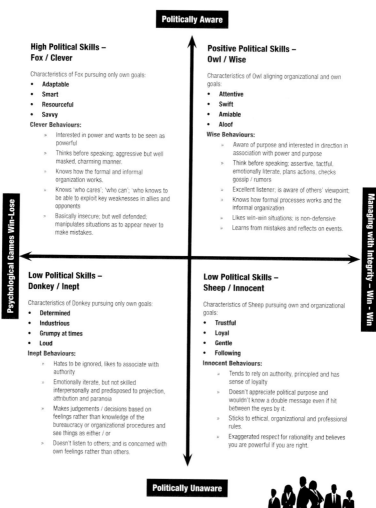

Politically Aware

High Political Skills –
Fox / Clever

Characteristics of Fox pursuing only own goals:
- **Adaptable**
- **Smart**
- **Resourceful**
- **Savvy**

Clever Behaviours:
» Interested in power and wants to be seen as powerful
» Thinks before speaking; aggressive but well masked, charming manner.
» Knows how the formal and informal organization works.
» Knows 'who cares'; 'who can'; 'who knows to be able to exploit key weaknesses in allies and opponents
» Basically insecure; but well defended; manipulates situations as to appear never to make mistakes.

Positive Political Skills –
Owl / Wise

Characteristics of Owl aligning organizational and own goals:
- **Attentive**
- **Swift**
- **Amiable**
- **Aloof**

Wise Behaviours:
» Aware of purpose and interested in direction in association with power and purpose
» Think before speaking; assertive, tactful, emotionally literate, plans actions, checks gossip / rumors
» Excellent listener; is aware of others' viewpoint;
» Knows how formal processes works and the informal organization
» Likes win-win situations; is non-defensive
» Learns from mistakes and reflects on events.

Psychological Games Win–Lose

Managing with Integrity – Win - Win

Low Political Skills –
Donkey / Inept

Characteristics of Donkey pursuing only own goals:
- **Determined**
- **Industrious**
- **Grumpy at times**
- **Loud**

Inept Behaviours:
» Hates to be ignored, likes to associate with authority
» Emotionally iterate, but not skilled interpersonally and predisposed to projection, attribution and paranoia
» Makes judgements / decisions based on feelings rather than knowledge of the bureaucracy or organizational procedures and see things as either / or
» Doesn't listen to others; and is concerned with own feelings rather than others.

Low Political Skills –
Sheep / Innocent

Characteristics of Sheep pursuing own and organizational goals:
- **Trustful**
- **Loyal**
- **Gentle**
- **Following**

Innocent Behaviours:
» Tends to rely on authority, principled and has sense of loyalty
» Doesn't appreciate political purpose and wouldn't know a double message even if hit between the eyes by it.
» Sticks to ethical, organizational and professional rules.
» Exaggerated respect for rationality and believes you are powerful if you are right.

Politically Unaware

Typical sheep believe you are powerful if you are right, very literal, and rarely know how to network or seek support. Sheep go where they are told and innocently follow their leader's direction without questioning. Sheep are dutifully loyal to an absolute fault. Even after being overthrown, Walker still had a sense of loyalty to Frank.

Donkey

If we look at the opposite end of the awareness and integrity scale, we will find the donkey behavior types. These behavior types are those with low integrity and lower awareness.

Donkeys are simplistic, insecure, and unprincipled in behavior. They have limited exposure to the world around them. Donkeys tell you what you want to hear if they can figure that out (often they cannot). They can say the right things but rarely appear authentic. Donkeys have an exceptionally low emotional intelligence. They are taken advantage of more often than sheep. Donkeys have limited values and no credibility. They are inept in behavior, focus on the end instead of the means, and cannot think far ahead in most circumstances.

If we look into the world of popular culture and television, we do not have to look far to find someone exhibiting donkey behavior. A quintessential donkey example is Homer Simpson of The Simpsons. Despite having a deep sense of loyalty for his family, Homer is rude, ignorant, and often taken advantage of by the outside world. He falls asleep on the job, his boss ignores him, and he neglects many of his responsibilities. You can blame the writers, but over the years, Homer's intelligence has declined significantly. He is a classic (yet cherished) oaf.

One time I was working with a client in Rochester, New York.

Their staff was genuinely nice. They hired a consultant to assist them with operations. He was pleasant, but during my auditing visits, I would try to guide him and help him with tasks. I needed certain reports, and it was his responsibility to send them to me. After two months, he still had not sent me the reports. When I contacted him to ask about the delay, he said it was almost done. "I will have it in a few days," he told me.

A few days went by, and I contacted him again. "I'm almost done," he told me again. However, he told me this a few days ago! In his mind, he thought he could make excuses and get away with not doing the report.

This is an example of donkey behavior. It is much better to be honest (high integrity) than to make excuses for the situation at hand. I tried to tell the owner of the company that their consultant was not helpful, but they didn't listen to me. The company wanted to give this guy a fair chance. That was their prerogative.

However, think about your own life. Have you ever blamed a technical malfunction for the lateness of a report or document at work? Have you ever said, "Oh, I did not get the email yet? My Outlook must have malfunctioned." These are acts of low integrity.

Typical donkey behaviors include those who are emotionally selfish, are inner-goal oriented, try hard to be nice but just don't know how to, and are unaware of their surroundings. They are clueless. Unlike sheep, they can act kind of dumb.

Fox

What happens when you mix high political awareness and low integrity? You get the fox behavior. These people are very aware of all things. They can spot sheep and donkey behaviors a mile away. Foxes are cunning. They know how to manipulate people. You often see fox types in the office setting. Foxes stand behind the scenes and push their own agenda through someone else (typically, sheep or donkeys). Foxes create secrecy, fear, and doubt. Fox behavior types want to be perceived as powerful. They exploit weaknesses to their own advantage.

We can find one of the truest depictions of the fox behavior in the television show, *Game of Thrones*. Okay, let's face it, there are quite a few foxes in that series, but one particularly stands out: Littlefinger, a.k.a. Petyr Baelish.

Baelish gets other people to do what he wants without them knowing he influenced their decision. He does not try to convince anyone of anything. He'll plant seeds of doubt and allow whoever he is trying to manipulate to make their own decision. Little do they know that he's already swayed their decision. Baelish is patient and cunning. He knows, like all foxes know, that when someone makes their own decision, they tend to stick with it.

Think about a time you asked your mother for something you knew she would probably say no to. Did she ever say, "Do whatever you want"? No, but she used a tone of voice that meant you could not do whatever you wanted. In fact, whatever you wanted somehow magically became "never mind." That is a fox behavior (though growing up it may have prevented us from doing some dangerous things).

Lord Baelish never lets his ego get in the way of his goals. When he tells Sansa Stark (Sophie Turner) he is going to give her away to the Boltons, she quickly fights back, threatening to starve herself. Lord Baelish responds with, "I won't force you to do anything. Don't you know how much I care for you?" In the same breath, he provides reasons why what he wants is the best plan (without coming out and saying that directly). Thus, he leads people (in this case, Sansa) to believe they are making a decision on their own. The decision ends up being exactly what he wants.

Foxes never give away their endgame. They just carefully play people like pawns in a chess match until they get the outcome, they have been seeking all along. Foxes are patient and cunning. They prey on sheep and donkeys, taking advantage of their low political awareness.

Based on the characters we've discussed so far; can you name another fox we may have mentioned earlier? That's, right . . . Frank Underwood from *House of Cards*. In Season One, Episode Six, there is a scene with Frank Underwood and lobbyist Marty Spinella (Al Sapienza).

The two men are located in an office at the White House. Frank sits at a long conference table, while Marty, holding his briefcase, stands across the room. Marty is running a successful teacher's strike across the nation. He strongly opposes pieces of Frank's education bill. Things are going well for Marty. He has the upper hand, and Frank needs him to fail in order to succeed. Little does Marty know that he's about to fall prey to a fox.

Frank begins by telling Marty he will never be powerful but will only work for powerful men (like Frank). He provokes Marty and his ego, eventually rising out of his chair. Marty backs toward the door. Frank continues his egotistic slurs, putting Marty in his place, intimidating him as he slowly invades Marty's personal space.

Frank has Marty pinned against the office door. He raises his arms and places them on either side of Marty's head. Marty firmly tells Frank to back off, but he does not listen. After pleading again for him to back off, Marty throws a fist in the air, connecting with Frank's jaw. Frank topples down to the ground, clutching his face and smiling.

Frank, the fox, got exactly what he wanted. He now has blackmail he can use against Marty should he interfere with Frank's education bill. All he had to do was trigger his ego and get a rise out of him. Marty followed through with the rest of the plan, just as Frank had hoped.

Eventually Frank rises and antagonizes Marty, causing him to have an outburst. Frank enters his physical space and completely controls the situation and argument at hand.

The greater awareness we have of fox behaviors, the more likely we can avoid falling into their well-concealed traps. Typical fox behaviors include not displaying feelings spontaneously, asking "what information do I have or need?" checking in on gossip and being insecure but well defended. Foxes enjoy games that have clear winners and losers. They like to win, obviously, and will do so almost every time.

Owl

The last category is a behavior we should all strive to emulate. The owl behavior is one with high integrity and high political awareness. Owls know what is always going on around them. Their role in leadership is to expose foxes and protect sheep and donkeys. This is how owls become credible leaders. Owls can cope with being disliked and have excellent emotional intelligence and interpersonal skills. They are excellent listeners and really listen, rather than just pretending to listen. Owls negotiate and operate with honesty. Owls are wise.

Taking a pause from our movie and television show examples,

a notable owl is Martin Luther King Jr. MLK was a man with great integrity. He was constantly provoked throughout his life. People consistently tried to get a rise out of him. They wanted to blackmail him. They wanted to shame and defame him. No matter what was thrown in his direction, MLK persisted. They arrested him. They punched him in the face. They bombed his home. He was tested every day but stayed true to himself and true to his vision until the day he died.

MLK was always looking for the win-win. He did not imagine a world where African Americans were superior to whites. He imagined a world where everyone was treated equally. His lifelong quest for equal rights is a permanent reminder of how an owl type should behave.

Owls are unshakeable. They possess the highest level of political awareness, and we should strive to be owl-like in our personal and professional lives. Typical owls are aware of purpose, are not defensive and are at ease learning from mistakes, are open and comfortable sharing information, and like win-win situations. Owls are looking out for everyone's best interest. Owls make the best leaders, though they can be hard to find sometimes.

What behavior do you exhibit or identify with? Are you innocent and naïve like a sheep? Are you blind and inept like a donkey? Are you cunning and ruthless like a fox? Or are you wise and just like an owl? Chances are you are all these. But a greater understanding helps us navigate our world a little easier. Increased awareness helps us strive for greater integrity.

Spotting the Icebergs

When understanding the dynamics of these four behaviors, they become easier to spot, especially in the workplace. Our awareness opens our eyes to icebergs. These icebergs are metaphors for issues at hand. We only see the tip of the iceberg protruding from the surface. We sometimes cannot recognize there is a massive iceberg beneath the surface. From an organizational standpoint, some things are apparent, but the underlying corporate culture may be like the rest of the iceberg, hidden from the untrained eye.

I experienced this while completing an audit in Cleveland, Ohio. It was the last day of the audit, and we were down to the last hour and a half of my visit. I had to leave in exactly ninety minutes in order to be on time for my flight home. The quality manager, Heather, had been working with me over the past few days. She was tall, with long brown hair kept high in a bun. She had pale skin and brown eyes. She was delightful to work with, very accommodating.

She kept saying things like, "I like your style. We are on the same page. You are so thorough." I was accustomed to compliments like these. I didn't not think much of them.

"Mr. Raza, we have a new person, Todd, who now works in our supply evaluation area. Would you complete an evaluation, please?" Heather asked me. "We would love to know ways we can improve. I'm sure there are things we can improve there."

I got a sense Todd maybe did not agree with Heather on certain things. I looked at the clock. If I spent thirty minutes evaluating the supply evaluation area, I would still have time to wrap up the audit and get to my car on schedule. I agreed to look over the area.

Heather made a list of equipment for an evaluation. She had three that needed review.

"I have thirty minutes, Heather. Then, I must make a judgment and move on to the final stage of the audit," I told her.

I surveyed the area. The supplier risk profile was not well defined, but everything else was in order. It was not a big deal, just a minor nonconformance. I shared this with Heather, and she pressed me to investigate the area further.

"No, I think we can move on now," I assured her.

Heather continued to press me, making the minor nonconformance seem like a much bigger deal than it was. I told her we must move on to the next area.

"George slipped out for a second. That is his area. We'll have to wait for his return," Heather said.

I looked at the clock. I had twenty minutes left.

"Heather, not a problem. Let's do a walk-through, and then George can explain whatever he needs to upon his return."

Reluctantly, she led me to the manufacturing floor. We took what seemed to be a detour to the area. Once we reached the floor, we started on the far-east side of the room and worked our way slowly to the door in which we entered.

I was about to wrap up when everything made sense. I spotted an issue. A critical equipment piece in the manufacturing process was being used before it received proper validation. This was a huge issue, a major nonconformance.

Heather sighed. Her plan had been foiled. She was hoping I would spend more time in the supply evaluation area and miss this egregious issue completely. With less than fifteen minutes left, I spotted it in the nick of time.

When I complete an audit, I am looking to see if you have the proper validations and paperwork needed, or if you don't have it. Heather was hoping not only to stall me, but to put me in the middle of a political tussle between her and Todd, the new employee. She wanted me to "school" Todd on best practices. That is not my job, and I did not fall prey to that plot. I could have easily made a mistake, but somehow, I did not.

People will distract you at all costs. The tip of the iceberg made it appear that the supply evaluation area concerned Heather. The middle of the iceberg revealed a political tussle between herself and the new employee. The huge base of the iceberg was the major nonconformance Heather hoped to distract me from finding. We must be able to see and spot these behaviors.

I have another great story about this topic. On another occasion, I was completing an audit in Oakland, CA. They led me into a large conference room. I tend to choose a seat in the room where my clients cannot see my laptop screen. Sometimes I may pull up information from another company's audit, and, if I am being honest, sometimes I take a quick peek at sports scores. Regardless, I always try to position myself in an area where I am the only one who can have eyes on my screen.

At this audit, I chose a seat facing a whiteboard. When I could do so, I like to use a whiteboard to provide a visual aid for my client. Remember, I like to teach my clients and guide them to tell me what I am looking for.

It was a particularly good audit, and everyone was friendly and professional. On day two, I was working hard when the boss of the company, David walked into the conference room. I looked up from my laptop only to see him scowl and storm out of the room. I was not sure what it was about, so I continued with my work.

I had some time before concluding the audit. I decided I wanted to use some of this time to speak with David. I was curious why he seemed so upset earlier. Everything was going well during the audit, so I could not pinpoint what might trigger him.

While talking with David, I told him stories of when I worked for a medical device company and we were audited. I shared stories of missing reports and simple mistakes, keying up my vulnerability. I even shared the Heather story with him (but omitted identifying details since my audits are confidential).

"I was almost deceived, but in the last few moments I found what I was—I guess—not supposed to find," I told him.

David laughed and ran his fingers through his black hair. He looked at me for a moment, slightly pensive, and smiled.

"You know, Salman, auditing is a science," he said.

"Of course, it is," I agreed.

"I work hard with my staff to create a strategy for entertaining our auditors," he said, shaking his head.

"How so?"

"Well, I told my team that the auditor should never sit in front of a whiteboard. They must always sit by the window."

"And why is that?"

"We want as many distractions as possible. If you are seated by an open window, there are many things that will draw your attention to the outside. You are more likely to miss something in our favor. If you are sitting facing a whiteboard, like you were, you have nothing to distract you. You can focus on every finite detail of the audit," he explained.

My rapport-building led him to lose his guard around me. I was grateful.

"I have never thought about that," I replied. I was happy he felt comfortable enough with me to share this information. It was something I would remember every time I chose a seat for an audit.

No one is perfect. We are all human. However, pursuing self-interest (or company interest in this case), people will stop at nothing to manipulate and distract you. They will try to trigger your ego. They will use mind games and tricks to get you to do what they want. You must be careful and carry a great deal of self-awareness with you wherever you go. Remember, we strive to be owls, not foxes and sheep or donkeys.

We will always make mistakes. We are human. But awareness of these mistakes, our behaviors, the behaviors of others, potential pitfalls, and intentions will help us accomplish our goals and establish trusting relationships in the long run.

Summary:

- *The Political Skills Model is broken into four quadrants:*
  - *Sheep: high integrity, low awareness*
  - *Donkey: low integrity, low awareness*
  - *Fox: low integrity, high awareness*
  - *Owl: high integrity, high awareness*
- *Throughout our lives, we can traverse throughout the different quadrants.*
- *When we understand the dynamic of these behaviors, they become easier to spot.*

Chapter 12: Establishing a True Heart-to-Heart Connection

Authenticity is the currency of trust. If there is no trust, can we even communicate with one another? In this chapter, I will explain the beauty of a heart-to-heart connection and how to foster authentic connections with those you interact with.

When we are kids, we spend time with other kids. Somehow, we find kids who share similar interests with us. We play games and develop an innocent connection with those around us. When we are adults, the same thing happens. We meet people in various settings, learn more about them, and want to spend more time with them. There is a moment when our hearts connect, like puzzle pieces. "Hey, I enjoy hanging out with this human." That is a heart-to-heart connection in its simplest form.

To build a trusting relationship, be it a business transaction or a lifelong partnership, we must channel our empathic nature to the highest degree. We must really feel others' feelings. We may not agree with them. We surely do not pity them. But we can get on the same emotional level and see eye-to-eye and heart-to-heart.

We cannot dismiss others or let bias or judgments cloud our vision. Remember: everyone has something unique to offer. Sometimes heart-to-heart connections are very intentional, and other times they are organic. The organic ones tend to catch us off guard.

Once, I had the rare privilege to experience a real and raw heart-to-heart connection with a perfect stranger. It was so unexpected, but so pure.

It was a warm summer day. I was sitting on a bench at our local playground watching my son, he was four. He was enjoying his imaginative world, pretending to be Thomas the Tank Engine, cruising through the playground. He was just living in the moment and the freedom that comes with being a kid with an uncontaminated imagination. I looked up at the sky. For once, we were having a sunny day in England. I could feel the warmth of the sun on my face. I listened to my son laugh, just a few feet away. It was a beautiful moment.

I was so caught up in the simplicity of it all that I failed to notice a woman walking toward me.

"May I sit here?" she asked me in a gentle voice while gesturing to the empty half of my bench.

"Sure," I replied, slightly startled.

I glanced at her: she was tall, with blond hair tucked under a wide-brimmed hat. She let out a small sigh as she took her seat, staring out into the playground.

We sat in silence. I did not think she wanted to have a conversation. It was not awkward at all.

"Dad, watch this," my son called out to me from the top of the red playground slide. He slid down, crashing at the bottom in a fit of giggles.

I smiled and laughed to myself. His joy was infectious.

"Is that your son?" the woman asked me suddenly.

"Yes, he loves playing here," I replied.

"How old is he?" she asked.

"He's four, about to turn five," I said.

We sat there quietly for a few minutes. Then, out of nowhere, my bench companion let out a slight sob.

"Julian would have turned five this year," she said, her voice shaking.

I was not exactly sure who Julian was, but I figured he was her son. I did not know if I should continue the conversation or not.

"Julian was my son," she finally said. She looked down at her wrist and thumbed a small gold bracelet with a locket charm. "He was playing in the front yard on a Saturday morning. His ball got away from him. Without hesitating, he ran out into the street. A teenager in a sports car was roaring down the block. He did not stop in time."

We sat in silence. I took off my sunglasses and looked at her. She turned to me, and our eyes locked. My brown eyes met her blue, tearful eyes. In that moment, I could feel her pain. It was as if someone stabbed an icicle into my heart a thousand times.

She held my gaze for what seemed like forever, but it was probably only a few seconds. I had never felt that way before. It shocked me. It was as if I could see into her soul. It was the most organic and pure heart-to-heart connection I had ever experienced with a stranger.

My heart continued to ache for her. I almost cried. My son continued to play, oblivious to the emotionally charged moment this stranger and I were experiencing.

"I'm so sorry," was all I could say.

She cried again. It was as if shards of guilt were tumbling

down her face with every tear.

"I looked away for one second. I could have stopped him," she whispered.

"I'm sure it wasn't your fault," I offered. "It sounds like it was an accident."

"It was, but as a mother, you're supposed to protect your children," she said.

"As a parent, I know that is our highest calling," I said. "But we're all just out there doing the best that we can."

I felt the pain in my heart subside just from talking and listening to her painful story and sharing my tearful eyes.

"I know. Thank you for letting me sit here with you today. My son used to love this playground too," she said with a slight smile.

"Of course. Anytime," I replied.

We sat there in silence while my son continued to play. Lunchtime grew near, and it was time to head home.

"It will get better," I assured her.

"I hope so," she replied.

As my son and I left the playground, he grabbed my hand and squeezed it.

"Who was that Daddy?"

"I'm not sure. She was a nice lady that needed a friend for a minute," I told him.

"That's nice," he said.

I smiled and felt like the most blessed person in the universe to have him in my life. I never got the stranger's name, but I know that moment we shared on the bench was one in a million. Those are the kinds of rare experiences that you never forget.

This story reminds me of the time at my life-changing

workshop when we sat in a circle and I somehow sensed the lady next to me would get up and hug the crying participant. That was another one of those rare moments I will never forget.

Through these experiences, I learned that we could feel the pain of others without knowing them. All it takes is a relatable connection and a nonjudgmental, open heart. If we learn how to be authentic, we can truly listen through the eyes, face, and heart. We can feel what is being said to us.

Heart-to-Heart Connections in Daily Life

So, how can we foster heart-to-heart connections in our everyday life? They may not be as extreme as this special encounter, but they are no doubt meaningful. This example is just a glimpse of what we can achieve.

I had a colleague, Evelyn, who I found annoying. She was cynical and overly critical of my work. No matter what I did, Evelyn would find something wrong with it. I would go above and beyond, and Evelyn would point out what I did not do. I felt like she appreciated nothing, especially if I was the contributor. It was so frustrating.

One day, I overheard Evelyn talking to one of our colleagues.

"The doctor called before lunch. Lung cancer," Evelyn said.

"Oh, I'm so sorry. What stage?" our colleague Margarete asked.

"Four. It is in his bones," Evelyn said, her voice shaking.

"I will keep your family and your little ones in my prayers. Let me know if you need anything," Margarete told her.

I did not understand. I saw Evelyn through a different lens. I learned she had two young children and was very fearful about what life would be like without her husband. I had to realize that Evelyn had something to offer. I had to recognize that the behaviors that left an awful taste in my mouth were just that: behaviors. Behaviors are not the person.

The next thing I had to do was ask myself if those negative feelings were true, or if I was just making them up in my head. Did I feel threatened by Evelyn? Did Evelyn remind me of someone negative in my past? I needed to see Evelyn as a person. We all need to see people as people, not as objects.

When we have negative thoughts about another human being, it contaminates our heart. It makes us unable to think properly or feel. Imagine you are driving down a highway, and your windshield is covered in dirt and debris. That is what negativity is like. What do you do? You put on your windshield wipers to clear it from your windshield so you can see properly.

If we walk around with a superiority complex, believing that we are better than others, then we form a tough layer of selfishness around our hearts. That layer prevents feelings of human connection and vulnerability from seeping in. That layer is a dirty windshield preventing us from seeing what lies in front of us. We need to clean the contamination of our judgments and prejudices from our hearts.

It takes time to acquire that "windshield washer fluid" to clear negativity from our heart windshield. The next time you harbor ill feelings towards a colleague or friend who has not wronged you check yourself. Ask yourself if the feeling is true. Is it valid? Try to find the root cause of that feeling. Do you feel threatened? Is your ego triggered? This self-awareness will help you paint a clearer picture.

Take small and genuine steps to be kind to that person. You

find that kindness makes you feel so much better than malice. It may feel awkward at first, but eventually you will find joy in your efforts. With a clear heart, you can see the talents and benefits every person has to offer the world.

This is important because this makes us human. When we treat people as humans, we establish a two-way communication. Empathy is a journey.

Tips for Establishing Heart-to-Heart Connections

Be Open: Unless you feel physically threatened (say, on a dark street and a stranger approaches you) - but always try to be open to interaction. Maybe someone asks you what time it is; give them the time with a smile. The gentleman who delivers the water jugs for your office cooler might teach you something, or maybe you both like the same football team! Have an open heart for people.

Take out those ear buds on your walk and smile at your neighbors. Ask the cashier how her shift is going instead of the generic "How are you?" Most people respond with an autopilot "good" or "fine." By asking a different question, you may get a different and genuine answer.

This was and possibly still is one of my weaknesses. It does not come to me naturally. I may come across as rude and arrogant to people. But I have trained my mind and I force myself to with the people around me.

Be Authentic: We have all heard the phrase "fake it till you make it." That does not apply here. People can spot a fake smile or fake interest from a mile away. One surefire way to disintegrate trust is to be fake. We must be authentic in our interactions. To be our purest and truest self is the best state to be. If it feels fake or flaky, it probably is. Sharpen your inner awareness and check yourself, to see if you feel less authentic when interacting with someone.

Be Empathetic: Empathy is the key to heart-to-heart connections. Empathy will set you free. Empathy is a map to treasure. Empathy! Empathy! Empathy! It is such a powerful thing — the ability to relate to and sometimes even feel another's emotions. Empathy allows you to establish common ground, lay a foundation of understanding, build upon bricks of trust, and get to the heart of another. If you are authentic, you will surely be empathetic.

Have a Grateful Heart: Years later, I still cherish that moment I had on the bench with that grieving mother. I cannot believe how vividly I felt her pain. It was as if I lost my son in that moment (thankfully I did not). The entire experience was moving, yet shocking and even a bit unsettling. However, I am forever grateful for it. Have a grateful heart. Grateful hearts are authentic and open. Always.

Summary:

- *Authenticity is the currency of trust.*
- *We must peel the layers of contamination from our hearts for a pure and authentic experience.*
- *There are four tips to remember when establishing a heart-to-heart connection:*
  - *Be open.*
  - *Be authentic.*
  - *Be empathetic.*
  - *Have a grateful heart.*

Chapter 13: Three Rules to Live By

We've covered quite a few topics so far and trying to remember them all may be overwhelming. To summarize some important aspects that we have explored, I would like to share with you three simple rules to live by. Hopefully, these rules will be easy to remember, and when you find yourself in a moment of conflict, you will manage the situation with ease and understanding.

Growing up, I found it easier to remember certain things by using acronyms. In the US, I have learned that students use PEMDAS—or "Please Excuse My Dear Aunt Sally"—for order of operations in math: parentheses, exponents, multiplication, division, addition, subtraction.

When I was in school, we used BODMAS. Instead of parenthesis, we say brackets. Instead of exponent, we say order, and the rest is the same. In university, they taught us a fun phrase to help us remember all the bones in the wrist. It was "She Looks Too Pretty, Try To Catch Her." It helped us remember Scaphoid, Lunate, Trapezoid, Pisiform, Trapezium, Triquetrum, Capitate, and Hamate/Hamulus. [27] For this chapter's lesson, I want you to try to remember RAN. Let's break it down.

R: Recognize the Challenge

One time, early in my auditing career, I was conducting an

---

27 "Wrist Bones," Mayo Clinic, https://www.mayoclinic.org/carpal-bones/img-20007898.

audit that woke up my human side. I was working with Finn, a likeable man in his mid-thirties. He was tall, very slim, with blondish brown hair and blue eyes. Finn was a simple man, not very well-spoken, but based on my early interactions with him, he seemed loyal and honest. He had been with this medical device company for about seven years.

Around midmorning, I suggested we take a quick coffee break.

"Oh, I don't really drink coffee, Mr. Raza, but the break room is around the corner, help yourself," Finn said with a smile.

I excused myself and made my way to the break room. Three of Finn's colleagues were there.

"Good morning, Mr. Raza, how is everything going?" the only woman in the trio asked me.

"We're off to a wonderful start," I replied. "Lots to do."

"At least Finn showed up on time," an older gentleman said with a smirk.

I gave him a quizzical look. Employee timeliness was none of my business unless it affected me personally.

"He's late almost every day. He used to be a real hard worker, but lately it is like he's barely here," the man said.

"Okay, well, thanks for the coffee," I said. I was not sure what to do with that information. On the one hand, it seemed like Finn's colleagues were trying to tell me not to trust in him. Maybe they were alluding to something more. For the time being, I put it out of my mind. Finn was here and on time, and we had plenty of work to get done. I returned, coffee in hand, and we resumed.

"Where is the production procedure outline?" I asked Finn while reviewing my notes.

"Oh, uh, it is not in the packet? I, uh, I will go find it, Mr.

Raza," Finn said nervously.

His colleagues' revelations popped back into my mind. I really did not see obvious reasons for slacking. He just seemed a little stressed and under pressure.

As I poured over the documents and files, I found something serious. A customer received an uncalibrated medical device. This piece of equipment takes a few hours to assemble. It listed the root cause as "oversight." In fact, "oversight" was listed as the cause in multiple areas of the audit.

The corrective and preventive action (CAPA) process states they must take appropriate actions for significant product and quality problems, identified from data sources. Based on my findings, they had not completed this important step in the process. It was a nonconformance.

Finn returned, document in hand. "Got it, Mr. Raza," he said triumphantly, a smile on his face. I am sure he knew about this nonconformance, but it was finally time to talk about it.

"Thank you. While you were searching for that, I discovered the missing CAPA step on the product delivered without calibration. Let's talk about that," I said gently.

"That? We fixed it. It was an oversight, well . . . by me, but we found the root cause and made a corrective action," Finn replied. The smile on his face had vanished.

"I understand, but oversight cannot be a catch-all for a root cause. The important thing is the customer returned the device, and no harm was done, but how can your company prevent this from happening?" I asked him.

"We fixed it. It is not is not a nonconformance. Please do not make it a major nonconformance," Finn begged. "My wife had a baby around that time, and we were up all hours of the night. It was a mistake."

I had been there. When my son was born, we had many sleepless nights. Sleep deprivation can lead to some serious errors in judgment and apparently a lackluster work performance. Finn was on the ball today, but based on his colleagues' comments, he had been struggling for a while. This nonconformance might just cost Finn his job. I could get him fired, just by doing my job.

"I will talk to my supervisor, and we'll work out the details," I offered. It was all I could say. I could not promise him anything, and I knew in my gut I had to do my job. But I also felt my humanity awaken. What happened to Finn could happen to anyone. We are perfectly imperfect human beings.

We worked through the rest of the process and wrapped for the day. Finn was nervous the entire day, subtly offering insights to his home life, showing me pictures of his daughter, and talking about how much he loves his job. I listened attentively and compassionately.

Back at the hotel, I talked to my senior colleague. I felt horrible.

"Salman, a nonconformance is a nonconformance. We have to write it up," he told me. "We can't turn a blind eye."

He coached me how to handle it. The important point was to take the nonconformance and present it as a learning opportunity. Instead of negative language such as "error," "fault," or "poor process," I would frame it as "teachable moment," "learning opportunity," "chance to improve," and "do better." He also suggested I set the groundwork to state that the nonconformance is a byproduct of a process issue, not a personnel issue. There were procedures that could be put in place to prevent incidents from happening. Finn was not the scapegoat; the entire company needed to be responsible.

In the end, we wrote the nonconformance. I delivered it in a manner of "teachable actions" instead of "things that were wrong." The company supervisors took our assessment to heart, and Finn did not lose his job. The company drafted a detailed corrective action plan, which documented each learning opportunity. We left no stone unturned. We emphasized that the root cause of the nonconformance was not an individual. The root cause of the nonconformance was inadequacies.

We would not have achieved this outcome if I wasn't aware of the environment and the challenge at hand. What if I took to heart what Finn's colleagues said? What if I did not approach my colleague with my feelings? Things may have turned out differently.

I have taken you on a few journeys where I had to recognize the challenge at hand. While in Alabama with the opinionated Colton Barns, I was constantly recognizing the challenge. I observed him and focused my surroundings (more on that next). I knew Colton would be angry if he received a nonconformance. Heck, I thought he might just kill me. However, I knew the challenge was to reach his human side. I had to find his humanity and, well, trigger it. That would be the key that could, and eventually did, de-escalate the situation.

Speaking of de-escalation, the North Carolina police officer… As he came to my driver side window, screaming at me, I sat there, nonplussed. I knew the challenge was not to challenge him. I recognized that a passive and polite demeanor would be the best course of action. As you know, thankfully, I was right.

What about when Judith wrote that email claiming I was not doing my job properly and shared it with my supervisors? If I had lashed out at her, I would have lost my job. Instead, I tried to empathize where she was coming from. I tried to walk in her shoes and guide her to an understanding. As you can see, this rule applies in just about any situation.

What can you do to recognize the challenge? The first thing you can do is train yourself to see the hidden signs. Be on the lookout for tone of voice, body language, body proximity, and eye contact. The next thing you can do is channel your empathy. My human side woke up when Finn shared his experience with his newborn. Be attuned to the things that wake up your human side. The third thing you can do is listen. When faced with any situation, often we talk first and, while "listening" to the other person, we are determining what we want to say next. When you pause and really listen, it might surprise you by what you can find out and what challenge you can uncover.

A: Be Aware of Your Surroundings

Throughout this book, I have encouraged you to be aware of many things: your body language, your tone, your ego, your motivation, just about everything. One more to add to the list is your surroundings. Like, when I was in that threatening audit in Alabama. What were some things I noticed? (Hint: the gun, the atmosphere, the way Colton carried himself.) These clues may have frightened me, but they also helped guide me to find a safe and neutral outcome.

Being aware of your physical surroundings is important, should you need to for a moment to clear your head. However, a conversational exit strategy is equally important. Sometimes you cannot physically leave the space. If that's the case, it is time to deploy the conversational exit. Do something to de-escalate the situation.

Tap into your own life! Find something non-conflict–related to talk about. It could be a television show or sports or even family. Often, I share stories of my children to neutralize the conversation.

One day I was working from home, and my daughter kept coming into my home office and saying hello to me. I always replied but did not take my eyes off the screen. By her third visit, she walked up to me, gently grabbed my face, and said, "Daddy, look at me. I just put on a new dress. You should say it is a pretty dress because it is." She looked beautiful, and I told her so.

My daughter teaches me so many things. Here she taught me how to live in the moment and appreciate the little things. Whenever I tell that story, my nervous auditees laugh and share stories and sometimes even photos of their own children. It is a great neutralizer, and it brings out the human side in all of us.

An audit can be a nerve-wracking experience for many people. I once had to monitor an intricate manufacturing process. While observing a female employee, I noticed that she was nervous. Her hands were shaking! I mean, who would enjoy an audit entourage examining your work? It would escalate the fear of judgment and the anxiety around letting your company down. It definitely was for her.

As soon as I noticed her shaking hands, I shared a delightful story about my daughter. While watching television, my daughter commented, "Daddy, the princess has such pretty nails!" I did not even notice the princess had nails! She kept talking about nails for most of the weekend.

So, instead of telling the employee I noticed her shaking hands, I told her it embarrassed me to admit I noticed her beautiful nails, thanks to my daughter. She smiled, laughed, and shared a story about her son. It was a great human moment. Right after our lighthearted conversation, she confidently showed the process, all while joking about the importance of her nails. We completed the audit successfully, and the employee felt more at ease with the entire experience.

If you do not have family or friend stories to share, or if you do not feel comfortable sharing personal information, look at your physical surroundings for a talking point. Perhaps it is a unique painting on the wall or a coffee mug design. You will always find something else to talk about, to neutralize the situation.

I cannot stress enough how important awareness is. Be aware of others, be aware of yourself, and be aware of your surroundings, both physical and conversational.

N: Never React, Always Respond

Hopefully, you will have remembered rules one and two before you get to rule three. However, rule three is equally important. Most of us, initially, do not appreciate the difference between "react" and "respond." Most people perceive them as different words with a similar meaning. However, if you think carefully, reaction is almost always impulsive. You see a funny movie, and you react by laughing. Someone yells at you, and you react accordingly.

But a response is measured and calculated. Response is being yelled at, pausing for a moment, and responding calmly and thoughtfully to the accusation. When we react impulsively, we react out of a triggered ego/anger/frustration/displeasure. We say things we do not mean. We do things we later regret. But if we somehow train our brain to always pause when we hear, see, or feel something we do not like, we can almost always just take a deep breath and follow rules one and two.

Let's talk about the North Carolina police officer again. What if I was combative? What if I shouted back as he shouted at me? I knew I did nothing illegal or wrong, but had I reacted impulsively, I could have gotten into serious trouble. Or what about my reaction and response to Judith? Remember how I typed the email out first, feelings and all, and then wrote a constructive and respectful response? I switched from a reaction to a response.

There are many things you can do to avoid reacting impulsively. You can write down your feelings and then discard the evidence. You can talk to a trusted friend or colleague before addressing an issue. You can count to ten before deciding. It may sound cliché but counting to ten really works! Ten seconds may be all you need to refocus. It is particularly important to practice this before you end up in the situation where you need it most.

This skill that will take time to master. We must gradually teach ourselves to put the brakes on our impulsive human nature. When we make a mistake, we must acknowledge it, even if it's after the fact. Each mistake rewires our brain, and that is a good thing. Each mistake serves as a teachable moment, giving us insight that we will use in the future.

Situational Rules for Consideration

I would not call these "rules to live by," but rather situational rules. Here are a few extra thoughts to consider:

Return to Neutral Ground

Only in times of conflict will you need to return to neutral ground. One of the best ways to accomplish this is to employ one of the conversational exit strategies mentioned above, to pull the participants out of the emotionally driven, heated conversation and into a positive and relatable one—even if just for a few moments.

If you were walking through a foggy forest, neutral ground would be a clearing. Neutral ground allows us to put the feelings aside and refocus our hearts and minds. It is important to note that neutral ground does not mean neutralize. This does not mean to back down and keep your feelings to yourself. Instead, it just means to neither agree nor disagree, to not take sides. Reinforce

What Is Agreed Upon

In any contradicting conversation or conflict, you will want to reinforce what is agreed upon.

Here is a great example. Medical device companies must register their devices with the regulatory authorities such as the Food and Drug Administration (FDA) in the US or a CE mark, by an authorized organization in Europe. Once registered, the medical devices are labeled accordingly.

While completing an audit, I discovered the company had a label with a different company address affixed to their devices. The name and address on the label needed to match the name of the company as registered with the regulatory authorities.

"Excuse me, but these labels do not match," I told Oliver, the staff member I was working on the audit with.

"Yeah, you're right, it does not look right," Oliver replied. "I better tell senior management."

He left to inform management and returned almost immediately with his supervisor.

"Where does it say that?" his supervisor demanded in a

defensive tone.

"Well, your information is inconsistent. The name on the labels does not match the name of your company," I replied.

"No, I can put any legal address on the labels," the supervisor said.

Actually, he could not.

"I'm just asking a question. I will write a report later, and you have time to investigate," I replied calmly. "I'm not writing a nonconformance . . . today . . . but we disagree on an interpretation."

"I don't understand," the supervisor replied defiantly.

"Okay, look. Let's assume a husband and wife are in court arguing about custody of their children," my colleague Lee offered. "Another person walks into the courtroom and starts adding commentary to the argument. The judge asks, 'Who are you?' The man replies, 'I'm a husband, too.' Everyone in the room says, 'No, you are not.' The man presents the judge with a paper stating he is a husband. The judge affirms his status of a husband but states it is not to the lady in question. 'You don't have any rights to use your husband status in this case,' the judge says. So, in your case, the address may very well be a legal address, but the contents within your registration papers and label must be married together and match. Don't be that random guy in the courtroom."

"I see," the supervisor said thoughtfully. "Odd example, but I get it."

Agree to Disagree

I gave him time to investigate the proper procedures for medical device labeling. He backed off the challenge and accepted the additional time. He did not admit fault. I did not agree to let it slide. By returning to neutral ground and reinforcing what they agreed upon, we both left feeling positive about the future. We agreed to disagree.

Reinforcing what is agreed upon also clears up any confusion that may remain. This reduces the chance for misinterpretation and future conflict on the same issue.

Put it all together and you have RAN, which is humorous. I hope you don't run anywhere unless you are in a physically dangerous situation. The foundation of RAN boils down to awareness, empathy, and communication, and practice makes perfect.

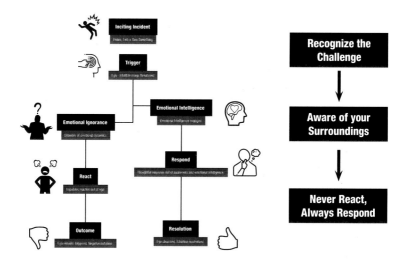

At the end of it all, sometimes the only thing you can do is agree to disagree. If you have tried everything and nothing seems to work, this may be the final step. I have had to agree to disagree many times. The resolution may not offer the complete sense of closure you would like, but at least it provides a denouement to the situation or conversation so all parties can move forward in whatever direction they choose.

Summary:

To remember many of the concepts we've covered in this book, memorize RAN:

- *Recognize the Challenge*
- *Be Aware of Your Surroundings*
- *Never React, Always Respond*

Chapter 14: Alabama Case Study

Now let us time travel for a moment. I would like to take you back to Alabama, and Colton Barns. From my initial phone call with him, to the moment my life was spared by heading to the airport, I applied a lot of the theories, rules, and ideas we've explored in this book. I present to you a case study.

Inciting Incident

Let's start with that phone call.

"You wanna get an earlier flight in, and I will pick you up from the airport?" Colton Barns asked.

"That is unnecessary," I replied. "I am getting in late, but I will rent a car and drive to you."

"Naw, I got you. Call me when you land," Colton argued in a distinct Southern drawl.

"Meeting" someone for the first time over the phone presents some challenges. First, I could not see Colton's body language. I can only go by his tone of voice and choice of words. Second, he cannot react appropriately to my body language. All we have is what we hear. It is up to us to read between the pauses, vocal inflections, and chosen language. With those limited communication resources, it is quite easy to misinterpret something.

Like a blank page, my first interaction with Colton helped shape my perception of him. I could tell he had a dominant personality. I sensed he may be on the lower end of the emotional intelligence spectrum. My next exchange led me to this conclusion:

"Say, where you from? You have an accent," he abruptly asked me, changing the subject.

It was a question I was used to.

"I'm from the UK," I answered.

"Really? Does not sound like an English name!"

In some contexts, Colton's inquiry might be construed as rude. It was a sharp pivot in conversation and slightly personal. Granted, we know I am used to such inquiries because my accent is very obvious, but Colton's contribution to our exchange led me to believe he really wasn't thinking before he was speaking. Perhaps he was an extrovert. Perhaps he was not aware how invasive his question was in a business conversation.

"You guys just had the Brexit. Things are really going to change around your land. They are kicking immigrants out. Policies are favoring those who were there first. I bet Spain and Germany will see big changes too," he said proudly.

I could have fallen prey to that trigger. I knew more about Brexit than Colton did. I had more experience on the subject. I almost felt defensive. I wanted to tell Colton he was mistaken and explain to him the true immigration implications of Brexit.

However, I stopped myself. I fell upon my emotional intelligence. I could see the conversation play out in a combative nature. There was no reason. I had nothing to prove. I had nothing to gain by telling Colton he was wrong. I knew he was wrong, and I was at peace with that. Therefore, I avoided a trigger.

The exchange led me to our first letter of RAN—Recognize

the Challenge. I knew Colton would be a different kind of client. I knew I would have to be careful with how I communicated with him and how I conducted the audit. He was going to be the type of guy who has a hard time taking no for an answer. In short, a nonconformance is sort of like a "no." It is really more of a "not yet," but clients see it as a "no."

The challenge was easier to recognize because Colton and I appeared to be on two different sides of the political spectrum. Sometimes it is easier to spot social cues when you disagree with the other person's opinion.

We might miss those cues and clues if we shared the same opinion. What if someone who was more culturally aware than Colton was in his position? They could massage my ego and tell me what I wanted to hear. I would get comfortable, thinking, Oh great, this person and I agree on the subject.

When two people think they agree, one person can easily turn the page and manipulate the other person. A more culturally sensitive Colton with alternative motives could have tried to put me in a position where I let my guard down. Then they would strike.

With this knowledge in mind, I knew I would be working with a political, strong, and opinionated client. That was my challenge. As our phone call ended, I began to think about what I would need to do to prepare for my visit.

First In-Person Impressions

As humans, we really should not judge. However, it is almost impossible not to. Our brain takes in our observations and processes it based on what we have previously been exposed to. As I drove into the strip mall parking lot where Colton's business was located,

I could immediately tell it was an odd place for a medical device company. I noticed the gun store and the janitorial supply store on either side of Colton's company. Prime real estate.

I walked into the office and noticed the smell, the dirty carpet, the drab atmosphere. Then Colton strutted out of his office without shoes on. My mind took all these sensory details and made sense of them - in a judgment.

I had to remind myself of the icebergs. Perhaps this first impression was only the tip of the situation. Perhaps I would be proven wrong about Colton and the state of his business (I wasn't). But I had to keep an open mind from the start. There was more to Colton than a shoeless businessman. And indeed, there was.

Oh, and let us not forget that horrendous bathroom.

Awareness of Surroundings

As they led me into Colton's messy office, I noted my surroundings. Everything was in disarray. Knowing Colton may have a strong temper based on our phone conversation, I was careful not to disturb anything in the office as I took my seat. On top of all this hyperawareness, I noticed his shotgun.

It was time to do a self-inventory of my feelings. I was feeling a little fearful. On the intensity scale, my fear was probably a three or a four. I did not fear for my life yet, but I was aware my client had a strong temper and a firearm was in his reach. So far, nothing gave me clues that Colton might use it against me. I knew I had to be careful.

Side note: Now, seeing a firearm out in the open may mean nothing to you. Perhaps you are used to this, or maybe you have firearms out in the open. To me, my fear was genuine. I have never seen firearms casually leaning against a wall before. I knew it was legal, but I was not expecting to see it. My mind perceived it as a threat. It was an enormous deal to me.

My back was toward the door. I had a clean exit, minus some obstacles on Colton's floor, if things were to get dangerous.

Trigger Fingers

With each question, Colton had an answer. But these answers were not the ones I was looking for. Instead, he had an excuse or blamed someone else for his company's shortcomings.

"The clean room got shut down because of Obama," Colton said. "It is his fault. The FDA inspector said they were here on executive orders from the president, and that is why they had to shut me down."

In Chapter Six, we discussed how the ego is triggered when one's own perception of an infallible image is threatened. Colton was triggered by the clean room situation. It was a minor trigger, or perhaps the very first trigger, but by asking about the clean room shutdown, I prompted Colton to offer an excuse as to why it happened.

I never would have expected Obama to be the scapegoat on this one, but he was. Metaphorically, Colton was caught with his hand in the cookie jar. But he was not willing to take responsibility for that, or any of his company's shortcomings. Colton had a reason for everything.

Colton in the Box

From that point on, Colton was in the box. He felt threatened. He felt wronged. He felt he was right, and no amount of missing documentation, or improperly labeled paperwork would convince him otherwise. Colton did not know he was in the box. I bet he never heard of Anatomy of Peace, but I could be wrong. Colton had nothing to gain by offering me excuses. I'm not sure he realized that.

Although, he may have. Shortly after the "blame game," Colton switched topics and tactics. He used Obama as a gateway into the future of American political affairs.

"Things are finally going to change, now that we got the right man in the Oval Office. Don't you agree?" Colton asked.

"I'm glad you feel that way," I replied carefully.

It could have been a trap, a way to get a rise out of me, a way to trigger my ego. I would not take the bait. Instead, I remained neutral. I practiced my N of RAN—Never React, Always Respond. I would respond to Colton, confirming I heard him and letting him know in the least patronizing way I could muster that "glad you feel things will be favorable for you now."

I would not agree with him. I would not disagree. I would affirm his feelings and attempt to move on. I needed to be sure my body language, tone of voice, and facial expressions matched the attitude I was trying desperately to present to Colton. I made firm eye contact. I smiled. I sat tall and confidently. I kept my voice at a conversational level.

Colton did not quit. I was not playing his game. He tried a new tactic by casually mentioning his association with soon-to-be US attorney general and former Alabama senator, Jeff Sessions. I glanced at the gun again. Time for another feeling inventory. Status: nervous and elevated fear. My palms were getting sweaty. I was determined not to crack, but as a brown immigrant, I knew what these kinds of casual remarks insinuated. I swallowed hard and tried to maintain even and steady breathing.

Mercifully, Colton, temporarily kicked me out. I was relieved to work with Betty. I could tell he was getting upset with me, partly because of the insufficiencies I kept inquiring about throughout the audit, and partly because I wasn't falling prey to his manipulation game. If he was trying to exert some control over me, I was not letting up that it was working, even though it kind of was. Perhaps he was just oblivious.

Don't Poke the Bear

Unfortunately for me, Betty was no help at all. She continued to call for Colton every time she did not know the answer. With each yell into his office, I held my breath. Do not poke the bear, Betty! He was already frustrated about the clean room shutdown. I did not want to provoke him even more. But Colton was not fazed. He curtly answered Betty's questions or told us to give him a few minutes while he would dig up the answer. I knew Colton's company was in for a nonconformance. There was no way things would pass as they were. Colton would not take no for an answer.

With Betty, I strived to ask her the right questions. "Why" questions were off the table. Yes and no questions were too simple and often met with an "I don't know." I settled for "where." Betty, can you show me where I can find the purchasing number for this order? Betty, can you show me where to find the proper documentation for this? The results were minimal, but it kept me from reaching a dead end with every question.

Promising Panera

Leaving the work area was liberating for many reasons. The first, obviously, was due to the clean restroom awaiting me at the restaurant. The second was that a restaurant is a public place and a neutral zone. I was not on Colton's turf anymore; I was at a recognized establishment. Ever aware of my surroundings, I made sure my back was to the restaurant exit so I could swiftly scoot out if a confrontation occurred.

Colton asked me questions that made me uncomfortable. The questions were where I am from and how I do not "look" like a typical British person. While I gave him a small token of personal information (my birth country), I deliberately switched the conversational focus off me. Talking about my upbringing or heritage could provoke another political conversation. Also, I did not want to feel uneasy over my lunch. Instead, I turned the focus back to Colton.

"Have you always worked for yourself? Or is this the first time you have run the business?" I asked. It was a yes or no question that I knew Colton would expand upon. I needed to touch his humanity. I needed to find something I could use when I had to break the news of the nonconformance. I needed to get to the lower and thicker levels of the Colton iceberg. I hoped this question would lead me on an exploration. I smiled and kept a casual demeanor.

An Iceberg Melts

"Yeah, I used to travel a lot. I almost got divorced because of it," Colton said thoughtfully. It was the first personal and nonpolitical thing he shared with me since I arrived.

"Clearly you have worked your entire life," I said. "Why are you still working? Wouldn't you rather be enjoying retirement and playing golf?"

I sensed an opening, a disarming, if you will.

He looked down and then back at me. "Honestly, I owe this company to someone. You see, I promised my granddaughter that I would take care of her. So, I am doing everything I can to make this company stable and profitable. I want to give it to her once it's back up and running with regulatory approvals for the US and EU."

The golden ticket! The way to Colton's heart! My ammo! That was it. I could easily empathize with that goal. I have children myself, and while I am not leaving a company for them, I do want what is best for them. I hope to have grandchildren someday. I would love for them to be secure in life, too. I could use this information and reengage Colton without triggering his ego again. I was thrilled with this discovery.

(Non) Judgment Day

The following morning, I did another feelings check-in. My feelings of apprehension had intensified, and I felt a sense of dread. I would be delivering bad news that day. There was no way around it. I could control the delivery, but the client's reaction would be out of my control.

I had learned a lot about Colton over that audit. I had a sense of what was important to him. He was a man with a lot of pride. When that pride was under attack, he resorted to blaming and excuses. He held himself (in his own mind) to an exceedingly high standard. Unfortunately, his surroundings did not match that standard. The condition of the offices, the inaccuracies in the paperwork and files, even the sweet but clueless nature of Betty were all the opposite of high standards. However, I was not there to judge. I was there to do my job, do it right, and get home to my family . . . alive. I knew I had to be far away from that shotgun when I finally broke the news to Colton. I also knew I had to present the information in a way where it felt less like failure and more like opportunity for the client.

A Near-Miss Trigger

I could not just cut to the chase and get out. Of course, I had to notice that Colton had his product on the shelf with my company's certification sticker on it. Another feelings check-in. I was feeling terrified, and my level of fear was reaching a high capacity. The last thing I wanted to do was trigger Colton again before delivering my news. But it was my duty to correct this issue since it was illegal.

"Your product has my company's certification sticker on it. This cannot be placed on your products until the audit is complete and you have received formal certification from us. This is illegal," I told him nervously.

"Ah, don't worry about that. We'll just take the stickers off for now," he replied nonchalantly.

A near-miss.

A Heart-to-Heart Connection

When the time came for me to deliver my results to Colton, I was anxious, fearful but also determined. I had a family that needed me. I would make it out alive.

"Let's forget about all of this audit stuff for a second," I said. "I really admire your desire and resolve to build this company. You are one determined and ambitious guy. You are quite noble in your intentions. I mean, you are preparing this company for your granddaughter. Who really does that type of gesture today? You are truly admirable and remarkable."

I meant it. If I did not, Colton would be able to sense my lack of genuine motivation from a mile away. I chose my compliments carefully and only shared truthfully. Colton raised his eyebrows. I continued.

"Based on the past two days, you know there are some things you are going to have to do. Let's make this company immaculate for your granddaughter. We want to make this company run smoothly and responsibly so your granddaughter says, 'What a great gift of life my granddad has given me.' Let's make this company the ultimate gift so your granddaughter believes you have changed her life with it."

Colton's face lit up. I could see his eyes start to water. We were connecting. For a moment, I was not the brown immigrant with the British accent telling him all the things wrong with his company. For a moment, I was just a man, recognizing the good intentions of another man and supporting him in those efforts.

"That is all I want," he said.

I explained the major nonconformities in detail but was careful to do so in a manner where each nonconformance sounded like an opportunity for improvement instead of "something is wrong." I was careful not to trigger his ego. I did not want him to feel like a failure; I needed him to feel successful, even in the face of a nonconformance.

"Everything will be fine once these things are taken care of. I know it does not sound good right now. It is unfortunate," I said. "Perhaps it is a blessing in disguise that this company was waiting for. There are a few major areas of concern. I will submit my report to the technical department. I have only summarized my assessment commentary. They will overrule my commentary if I have made mistakes. Someone from my company will get back to you."

With that, he gave me a handshake, and I was free to leave. My final feelings check-in: a bit shocked, a bit relieved, a bit in awe of what had just happened. These feelings were quite intense. Somehow, everything I learned about human interactions and egos came to play in my favor during this audit.

I recognized the challenge. I was constantly aware of my surroundings and my emotions. I never reacted to Colton's threats or presumed threats but always responded. At the end, I even employed "return to neutral ground." That is one audit I will never forget.

Summary:

- *Always keep your composure and use RAN*
- *Despite aggressive behavior, delay your judgement but never lose sight of your objective / task at hand*
- *Remember, beyond the out layer i.e. apparent undesired behavior, almost always there is a pure heart; once we find a way to connect to that pure heart, we can achieve the desired results.*

Chapter 15: Managing Passive-Aggressive Behavior

Early in 2018, the *Harvard Business Review* published an article titled "How to Deal with a Passive-Aggressive Boss." [28] The piece, written by Ron Carucci, gives readers concrete ideas on how to mitigate a passive-aggressive environment. The key tips are anticipate and prepare, don't stoop to their level, and respectfully call the question. Sound familiar?

We have certainly covered a few "rules" and suggestions throughout this book that contain elements of these three tips. They sound a lot like Recognize the Challenge, Be Aware of Your Surroundings, and Never React, Always Respond.

When you recognize the challenge, passive-aggressive behavior will not catch you off guard. You know it is about to happen because you've played out scenarios in your head to determine what your course of action will be.

If you combat passive-aggressive behavior with more passive-aggressive behavior, then you'll get nowhere. Passive-aggressive behavior manifests out of a triggered ego. The key is to find a way to disarm the other person's ego as well as your own.

Addressing the Behavior

Passive-aggressive behavior needs to be addressed for it to stop.

28 *Ron Carucci, "How to Deal with a Passive-Aggressive Boss," Harvard Business Review, January 24, 2018, https://hbr.org/2018/01/how-to-deal-with-a-passive-aggressive-boss.*

However, forcefully calling out the passive-aggressive individual will yield little to no results. The whole goal is to disarm the ego. When dealing with a passive-aggressive individual, remember that whatever they are feeling is true. That's right. Whatever they are feeling is true to them. All feelings are okay. All behaviors are not.

Let's say your boss is constantly critical of your work but never delivers any concrete feedback. She continually tells you what a bad job you're doing but she doesn't tell you exactly how or why. This is passive-aggressive behavior.

As your supervisor, she should guide you to the finished product and help you improve along the way. Instead, she is harboring some sort of ill feelings toward you. Maybe you remind her of someone in her past. Maybe there is something you do around the office that really annoys her. You may never know the real reason, but it is time to confront her about it.

Instead of calling her out on her behavior, talk with an even tone and request concrete feedback on your work. When we lower our own ego, we present ourselves as someone who wants to improve and do better. If we do not challenge the passive-aggressive individual, but ask for guidance, their ego will begin to disarm. They will (in most cases) come back to their rational self.

The Passive-Aggressor Within

What if you are the passive-aggressor? What are some ways you can recognize the challenge and disarm your own ego?

Passive-aggression bubbles to the surface when we feel we are in competition with someone. Perhaps we feel a colleague gets away with murder and is treated with great favoritism. Maybe it is because we bump heads with someone who has different viewpoints. The fundamental motivation is a sense of competition whether we realize it or not.

It was the 2014 FIFA World Cup, and Germany and Brazil were battling for the win in the first semi-final match. Germany scored four goals within six minutes and brought the score to 7-0 in the second half. With that advantage, would the German team play their hearts out? Would they leave everything on the field despite such a lead? The German players felt secure. When you're secure, you can think clearly. If you don't have to worry about the unknown, you stay focused. Brazil went on to score a consolation goal in the final minutes of the match.

When security is at stake, we challenge and fight harder. At least that is what John McEnroe did in 1981 at Wimbledon (and quite a bit afterwards). He famously challenged the umpire saying, "You cannot be serious!" Tennis is considered a civil game. People were stunned by his outrage and behavior. It was the line that was memorable, because when something is at stake, our human nature is to fight for control.

I receive performance reviews at least twice a year. In my early days as an auditor, I used to take my performance review, analyze it, and pick out points where I felt I had been wrongly graded. The system was simple. Your effort in certain tasks was rated four to one, with four being exceptional and one being poor. While doing a self-evaluation, there were a few areas I felt I did exceptional. I marked my grade as such. Upon the review, my boss said they were average.

I presented my case enthusiastically, but my marks remained unchanged. I felt my progression within my career and the company would be determined by this evaluation. I felt like I was in competition with my colleagues.

I found that very frustrating until I grew older and more seasoned in my work. The performance reviews were important, but their primary purpose was to motivate the employee to set goals for themselves. I realized that promotions and bonuses were not granted solely on the performance review.

I knew I was doing a good job. My clients were satisfied with my work, and that is what was most important to me. Now when I receive my performance evaluation, I take the scores given to me without a fight. On several occasions, I have rated myself a three and my boss gave me a four!

This attitude toward my performance evaluation does not translate into apathy. Instead, it translated into security. I am secure in my work and how I carry myself on the job. I know what my ratings are in my mind and heart, and to me that is what matters.

When we're secure in our mind and heart, we do not feel the need to challenge others. We rise above.

Security at the Airport

As I've stated, I travel a lot for my job. That means a lot of air travel. One way I pass the time when I'm not working is to people-watch. You see a lot of things when you people-watch in the airport. You see people run for flights. You see people sleep on floors. You see people line up a half hour before the boarding gate opens, eagerly waiting to get on the plane.

I usually sit there, waiting and watching.

As humans, we crave control. We don't like surprises (except maybe the occasional gift or random act of kindness). The passengers lined up early, waiting for the first call to board the plane, may be trying to ensure their carry-on luggage has a spot in the overhead bin. Often, people in later boarding zones will have to check their bags due to a lack of space in the overhead compartments.

Meanwhile, I'm sitting comfortably in the terminal, waiting for the line to go down. I feel secure. Why? Because I have checked my bags and I know I have a seat on that plane. I don't feel the need to get anxious, stand, and wait. My security makes me feel at peace.

The behavior of the other passengers is not necessarily passive-aggressive, but passive-aggressive behavior can be triggered by the fear of the unknown. The unknown shakes our feeling of control. Our response to the unknown is influenced by our personality types.

Judging types like to have things planned out. They don't like to rush or do anything last minute. Meanwhile, perceiving types are our "winging it" types, remember? They trust everything will work out. My brother-in-law has missed a flight or two simply because he waited to go to the bathroom until the last minute and just "had to go."

The bottom line is that we must find a way to let go and be at ease. One way is to ask yourself, "Can I change my immediate situation?" "Is this in my control?" If it is, make a three-step plan to change the situation. If it is not, take a deep breath and let it go.

It takes time to get into the habit of analyzing your thoughts, but with proper practice, you will be able to find ways to put your mind and heart at ease. Remember, sometimes it is for the best!

All in Interpretation

When there is a misunderstanding between two people, it may lead to passive-aggressive behavior. This happened during an audit I was supervising a while ago. We had a seasoned auditing veteran,

Lee, whom I previously mentioned, join our team. He had a lot of experience in auditing, but I was assigned to supervise and teach Lee the processes that our company employs for audits.

We were in Mexico for a business trip, and while working through the audit, Lee suddenly had a disagreement with the auditee. Our client was annoyed because she did not understand what we were trying to convey about her company, and a nonconformance was on the table.

The disagreement got a little heated with both the client and Lee raising their voices. Since I was the supervisor and a neutral person in the group, I stepped in and suggested we take a break. I worked with the client for another 20 minutes, and then we all decided to call it a night.

"I had it. I know what I'm doing," Lee said as we walked into our hotel.

"I understand, but as a neutral party, it was easier for me to step in and help her understand what we were asking," I replied.

He still seemed upset.

"Why don't you go over your procedures, and we'll start fresh in the morning?" I offered. Lee did not respond.

The following day was uneventful. Lee kept to himself and stayed out of the way. That evening I asked him to join me for dinner.

"You're awfully quiet," I said.

"I did not do anything wrong," Lee said.

"Oh, I never said you did. I just thought, since I'm supervising, I could take this situation off your hands," I replied.

It took me a few minutes to piece together why Lee was so upset. Turns out, he was upset with me. He thought that by telling him to take a break and go over his procedures, I was disapproving of his work. To him, my suggestion was punitive and reprimanding.

That was not the case, but Lee felt the integrity of his work experience was being threatened.

"Lee, it is still a nonconformance, you are right," I told him with a smile. "Don't worry."

"I'm confused. You pulled me out of the audit. I'm not worried about the nonconformance," he said.

I tried to explain why I excused him from the disagreement portion of the audit, but he was suspicious. I sensed he thought I was a hypocrite.

"We're going to have to explain to the client why it is a nonconformance and they need to accept that fact," I said.

"How are we going to do that? I did that," Lee replied.

"You did, but there are different ways to deliver the news. We'll tackle it together tomorrow. The key is to give them the news gradually, so they stay engaged, rational, and attentive," I said.

As soon as the client goes into defensive mode, the rational mind will stop working and will not listen. That is where passive-aggressive behavior comes from. That behavior creates unnecessary stress and strain.

"I feel like there is only one way to tell them it is a nonconformance," Lee told me.

"We will see about that," I said with a smile.

The next day Lee was skeptical, but I was determined to show him the magic. We entered a small meeting room where we'd be conducting the last part of the audit. Seated around the table were three senior employees. They had papers in their hands streaked with yellow from their highlighters. These people looked ready for a fight.

Among them was the Vice President of Quality and Performance. He was in his late fifties and wore what looked to be an expensive suit. He didn't attend the previous days of our audit, but we heard he drove in from San Diego to meet with us.

I could already sense the aggression growing in the room. I could read the body language of our clients — stiff, rigid, with furrowed brows and intense stares. These clients must have spent the evening doing their homework. While Lee and I were dining and sorting through our misunderstanding, our clients were trying to pick apart our nonconformance.

Lee's approach was not going to work.

I greeted Tim, the VP, and thanked him for driving all the way from San Diego to join us.

"How was your drive?" I asked him.

"Oh, it was fine, I crossed the border this morning. There was a bit of a line to get into Mexico, so that took more time than expected."

"I'm sure. Well, we had very productive days here!" I said.

Lee stood silently, watching our exchange carefully. I gave Tim the summary of the audit even though I guessed he'd already received a full report from his employees. I started by sharing all the good things we witnessed.

"You have a very competent team," I shared with him. "Very impressive performance. Your delivery is exceeding your target timeline. This is excellent."

I continued with a few more genuine compliments. I let him know I saw his company's journey from where they have been and where they are now. I sympathized with him because the company was frequently audited. It was almost death-by-audit for these people; no wonder they were frustrated.

"Each person that audits your company has a different set of requirements. That must be frustrating," I told him.

He nodded and smiled. I could tell the aggression and fight was starting to dissipate. He was starting to become Germany vs. Brazil in the 2014 World Cup. Everyone wants to please everyone, and it is almost impossible to please everyone.

"You have a great system, and everything is automated, but your procedure talks about paperwork," I said cautiously. "Your procedure mentions things such as pink slips and yellow slips, but you do not have any slips. Your procedure is misaligned. You have a far superior system than what your procedures portray."

I made sure he knew that I was not saying his system was wrong but rather that it was misaligned. Tim finally understood.

"We will write this as a nonconformance, but you just have to edit your procedures to align with your electronic system, and you will be good to go," I offered.

With the tension in the air dissipating and ego disarmed, in a similar way I slipped in more complex nonconformities, even though they were potentially more contentious. Since the egos were disarmed and the rational mind was at its peak, it was easier to talk about those issues. Of course, we continued to stay calm and keep repeating positive aspects and competence of individuals.

The company did not put up a fight, and we were able to do our job the right way. Lee was amazed, and he learned a lot. As we returned home, we had a chat and cleared the air. He admitted to feeling defensive, and I admitted to not realizing the misunderstanding my direction may have caused. Today, we're good friends.

Going Forward

Now you have a better idea of where passive-aggression manifests from. It stems from insecurity. It stems from competition. It stems from a lack of control. The key is to recognize these triggers both in yourself and those around you. As always, this takes time and effort. It is a lifelong journey, but with practice and patience, we will succeed.

Summary:

- *Passive-aggressive behavior needs to be addressed for it to stop.*

- *Passive-aggression occurs when we believe we are in competition with someone.*

- *When you recognize the signs of passive-aggressive behavior, it will not catch you off guard.*

Chapter 16: The Art of Advice

I was eleven years old. You know how eleven-year-old boys are. We're approaching puberty, our teenage years are on the horizon, and our boyhood is coming to a close. At least that is how I felt. It is a special age. An age where your mind, body, and heart are constantly changing. My dad observed and sensed these changes. He knew he would soon have to have an important conversation with me. No, not that "talk," but it was one of an adult nature.

I enjoyed playing make-believe with my little brother and a few friends on our street. You could usually find me playing the role of Marion "Cobra" Cobretti, taking names and saving the world. I would not see the movie until much later in life as it was rated "R." But I remember seeing the posters for the movie in my neighborhood. Sylvester Stallone looked so cool.

I would stand at the edge of the street, sunglasses on, a fake paper cigarette hanging out of my mouth. The game never got old. I felt so cool, pretending to inhale that paper cigarette and puff an imaginary cloud of smoke into the air.

Little did I know that my father was watching me. One day, as the sun went down, it was time to come inside and get ready for dinner. After dinner, I sat in the family room with my dad. We talked about anything and everything. He would ask me how my day was, and he was genuinely curious to know what was going on at school. I loved having these impromptu chatting sessions with my dad. On that at evening, we were talking about cricket, and then my dad changed the subject to something a little more serious.

"Salman looks like you were having fun playing today. You're really playing grown-up games now," he said.

"I was Cobra!" I replied excitedly.

"I see. I'm proud of you, Salman. You're getting into 'big-boy stuff' now. Pretty soon, you'll be a teenager."

I smiled. It always felt good when my father was proud of me.

"Being the hero is a noble role to play," he told me. "So, tell me about that fake cigarette you were playing with," he prompted.

"Oh, I just grabbed a piece of paper and cut it down. Then I rolled it gently. I took some black crayon for the burnt tip and stuck it in my mouth. Just like Stallone!" I replied, pleased with my handy work.

"Do you think smoking is cool?" my dad asked.

"It looks cool," I said.

"I thought so, too, when I was your age," he replied. "I was so fascinated by it. You inhale this small stick, and smoke enters your mouth and fills your lungs. Then it comes back up your throat and out your mouth again."

I sat there quietly and listened.

"I did not start smoking until later in my teen years, but it felt so neat, blowing smoke right out of my mouth," he said.

"You did not smoke at my age?" I asked.

"No, I waited, eagerly, excitedly, until it was legal for me to smoke," he said. "I remember when I bought my first pack of cigarettes. I think I was about 18. You know, smoking is for adults."

I was really enjoying this conversation. Here was my father, opening up to me about his love of smoking. I wasn't sure if I would love smoking, but it sure looked cool. I could feel my dad's emotions and excitement around the smoke coming into my mouth and into my lungs.

"Salman, if you decide you want to smoke someday, I cannot stop you. I would be a hypocrite because I smoked and enjoyed smoking myself. If you want to smoke, it is not a problem," he said. "But I want you to remember two things. First, I know you respect me and don't want to hurt my feelings, but if you decide to smoke, don't do it behind my back. Smoke in front of me."

I nodded. Eyes wide.

"Two, if you need extra money for cigarettes, don't ask other people. Come to me and ask me. It is okay."

I nodded again with a big smile.

"I have enjoyed smoking, but in my experience, it really is not a good thing. You get a few minutes of pleasure out of it and put your health at great risk," he admitted.

My father had a heart attack a few years prior. He ended up in the ICU and really had the scare of his life. He felt his time was up and we (his children) were far too young. He knew he could not afford to be irresponsible, so he quit smoking and made steps to get healthier.

I was confused. I thought maybe he was paving the way for me to smoke guilt-free when I got older.

"People will say you cannot be a man if you don't smoke. Boys will entice you. However, if you do not smoke, you will be a gentleman," my father said.

I was only eleven, but I made up my mind. I would not smoke.

My father had carefully laid out the choices and the consequences. He did not instruct me what to do in terms of smoking but laid all the cards on the table.

His transparency led me to make the right decision. When you give a person the choice to do something or not, you also give them ownership over their decision. That is exactly what my father did. That man-to-man conversation has had a lasting impression on my life.

Giving Advice

Advice is structured information that one person offers to anther to impact a choice or behavior. The most effective way to give advice is to offer someone a choice and present yourself as a neutral party. By leaving your bias out of the feedback, you create a judgment-free environment for the person you are trying to advise.

The first thing to remember is to check if the person you are offering advice to is ready to receive it. You can do this by monitoring body language, tone of voice, and demeanor.

A person in an elevated state of emotion (furious, terrified, depressed) might not be ready to receive advice. Their emotions are the loudest thing in the room. Emotions can steer us down a path of irrational behavior. Remember your icebergs: what you see at first may not be the whole of what is happening.

There are several tips you can utilize when giving advice:

Make the advice-receiver feel safe:

By avoiding defensive questions and passive-aggressive tendencies, you can help your advice-receiver feel safe to receive the advice. Avoid phrases such as "We need to talk" or "I have something important to tell you." That puts pressure on the moment. Instead, casually engage the individual in casual conversation and then move to your advice following these steps.

Offer advice on specific and observable behaviors:

My father noticed me playing with my friends and pretending to smoke a cigarette. This behavior was both observable and specific. Advice is well received when it is directed at a singular issue. What if my father tried to give me advice on smoking, girls, and preparing for college all in the same conversation? I would be confused and perhaps not take away his lesson as graciously as I did when we only addressed smoking.

Do not advise on personal characteristics or attitude:

Have you ever been upset in a situation and someone said, "You need to change your attitude"? How did that make you feel? In most cases, the ego would be triggered, and the person would get defensive. When you offer advice on personal characteristics or attitude, you are telling the other party that something is inherently wrong with them as a person. Changing your attitude is a lot harder than stopping or altering a troubling behavior.

Describe the observable behavior: Be as specific and direct as possible. Avoid "beating around the bush." Also, make sure you ask the right questions. If you ask someone, "Why do you do that?" you will put them in defensive mode. Perhaps say, "Could you share with me how this behavior makes you feel?"

Remember when I was at my sister-in-law's party? I sat there, watching the people mull about, thinking about my upcoming work week with a scowl planted on my face. My sister-in-law approached me and asked if I was upset with her.

"You look very upset," she said. "Did I do something to offend you?"

Her inquiry addressed my observable behavior. She saw me

scowling. She was worried she offended me. She wanted to get to the bottom of it.

"No, I'm just worried about work," I replied. "Everything is lovely."

I reassured her. This exchange reminded me to be cognizant of my facial expressions. What you feel on the inside is often displayed on the outside.

Describe the consequences of that behavior:

My sister-in-law expressed she was worried she offended me. My behavior was making her question her motives and her party.

Focus on behaviors that the receiver can do something about: I could obviously change my facial expression and be more aware of what mood I'm portraying.

Be direct:

My sister-in-law did not make small talk. She did not try to get information out of me by prodding me with investigative questions. She asked me point-blank what she needed to know.

Avoid generalizations and avoid the words "need to":

When we say, "need to," we automatically take the "choice" out of the advice. People shut down when they hear "need to." Very few humans on this earth like being told they "have" to do something. Keep the ego calm by avoiding those two words. She did not tell me, "You need to have fun." Instead, she thanked me for explaining myself and went back to entertain her guests, relieved I was not upset with her.

Be supportive and timely:

My sister-in-law could have told me months later that my facial expression at her party made her think she upset me. Instead, she confronted me right there in the moment. That was impactful.

Let's take a look at what this might look like in a work situation.

One of my friends shared with me a story from his work about two colleagues. Darian and Ronald worked for the same public relations company. The company was small, with about six associates and one president. Each week the president would host media pitch meetings where the team would share their ideas.

The purpose of the meetings was to generate press pitches to secure news coverage for the company's clients. The president would accept or reject pitches each week based on the ones she thought would generate the best results.

Companies on a larger scale, often meant more hours spent generating publicity for the client's company. For these clients, two associates were assigned. Darian and Ronald were assigned to a large pharmaceutical client. They spent the four months working as a team to generate press releases, new product announcements, representative interviews, and internal communications for the pharmaceutical company.

At the next pitch meeting, Darian grew frustrated.

"All right, Darian and Ronald, what is on deck for the next week for you guys?" the president asked.

"We have put together a comprehensive social media campaign that we hope will generate awareness for the upcoming product launch," Ronald said.

Darian sat there and nodded.

"We expect to see measurable results on Twitter specifically," Ronald said. He continued to provide a breakdown of the plan. It was approved. The president rarely had any concerns with Darian and Ronald's teamwork.

Except Darian did not feel like she was part of a team. Ronald made sure to speak up every meeting and report back on their work without giving Darian the opportunity to speak for herself. If she did not have other clients, she thought the president might think she was a mute. Ronald did not exactly take credit for their teamwork, but he never offered her the chance to speak in pitch meetings. It was time to do something about that.

After the meeting, Darian asked Ronald if he would swing by her desk to go over a few things for the social media campaign. She chose not to say "we need to talk" or draw any concern to her plan. Ronald came by, and after they felt they had their strategy in place, Darian finally spoke up.

"Ronald, for the past few months, you have done a great job sharing what we're proposing during our pitch meetings," Darian said.

"Thank you, that means a lot. It is a team effort," Ronald replied.

"Yes, it is a team effort, but sometimes I do not feel like I am on a team," Darian said gently. "You don't give me a chance to be vocal in our presentations. You often speak first and for me."

Ronald listened quietly.

"Perhaps you could turn the floor over to me or let me start our presentation every other meeting," Darian suggested.

"I had no idea," Ronald said. "I thought you liked that I wrapped our pitch points nicely."

"You do a great job, but for us to be a team, I need the opportunity to pitch in the meetings as well," Darian replied.

Ronald felt bad he was so blind to Darian's issue, but after this neutral and civil conversation, he made sure to offer the floor to her during pitch meetings. The president noticed an improvement in their team dynamic, and they went on to produce excellent public relations results for their client.

As you can see, Darian made Ronald feel safe by not blindsiding him or presenting formidable foreshadowing about what she needed to address. She chose to tack the feedback on at the end of a regular work meeting instead of a separate event. She addressed a specific behavior. Darian did not assume anything or try to label Ronald's behavior. She simply stated what she's witnessed and how it makes her feel.

Additionally, her timely address of the behavior helped the issue be top of mind. Ronald could recount the meeting they just had and see his behavior fresh in his mind.

Darian's direct, timely, and nonaggressive approach led her to get the results she needed.

Sometimes it may take time to establish a safe and trusting space when you need to give advice. My relationship with my dad was and still is a very special one. We have respect and trust each other. The working relationship between Darian and Ronald had been positive most of the time. The only issue was the one Darian addressed directly and at the end of a routine work brainstorm session. Always remember that trust takes time.

Throughout our lives, we will undoubtedly be in a position to receive advice. I would like to share some of the key elements of receiving advice.

The Art of Receiving Advice

Deepak Chopra tweeted sage advice: "For conflict resolution, treat your adversary with respect. Recognize perception of injustice on both sides. Recognize fear on both sides. Refrain from belligerence. Do not discuss ideology. Learn to forgive and ask for forgiveness. Understand emotional intelligence." [29]

The advice is beautifully written and truly authentic. However, people may argue that the recipient was in no position to openly receive such advice. Why? Well, Chopra did not meet the recipient where he or she was at. When possible, give and receive advice in a face-to-face, person-to-person setting. The advice exchange is more meaningful that way.

As an advice-receiver, what should we know?

Be receptive:

As the receiver of advice, remind yourself to be receptive. This is hard since it can trigger the ego. When someone gives us advice, our mind can think our "infallible image" is being threatened. If you're receiving advice, repeat to yourself, "I am open to receiving this advice. I will choose what I want to do with it." No one says you have to take all the advice. If that were the case, we'd have some very confused people walking around!

Avoid getting defensive:

If someone is giving advice from a good-natured and authentic place, the ego should remain asleep. Advice is never meant to be threatening. Advice should not come from a place where "something is always wrong." By repeating the mantra above, your ego will stay quiet and your defensive impulses will rest while you hear what the other person has to offer.

Listen with your heart:

To truly benefit from the gift that advice may bring, you must listen with your heart. Tune out distractions. Don't think about how you're going to respond right away. Listen to the words coming out of the advice-giver's mouth. Think about each word. Absorb the

---

29 *Deepak Chopra (@DeepakChopra), "For conflict resolution treat your adversary with respect," Twitter, July 31, 2018, 4:20 a.m., https://twitter.com/DeepakChopra/status/1024253586610561024*

advice. This will prevent a miscommunication.

Don't respond immediately:

After the advice has been given, do a feelings check-in. How do you feel? At what level of intensity are your feelings? What do you need to do to feel neutral or at peace? Perhaps it is to thank the person for the advice. Maybe it is to tell them you'll think about it. Maybe you need further clarification.

Have a conversation: Have a conversation about the advice. This will clear up misunderstandings. It could deepen the level of advice you're receiving. Or perhaps you've decided the advice is not for you. A meaningful conversation will help, regardless of the choice you decide to make.

Appreciate the feedback:

Good advice or bad advice is a gift. You may choose to regift, throw away, or keep, but you must thank the advice-giver for the advice. Don't resist that gift. Don't reject that gift. A simple thank-you and recognition will go a long way. When you receive feedback, don't try to explain yourself. That will take away from the moment. Just accept the gift and choose what you wish to do with it.

As auditors, sometimes, we are audited by auditors. Once while working on an audit in Garden Grove, California, I was audited by a Canadian regulator. Most auditors experience this throughout their careers. The purpose is to make sure that I'm following best practices and conducting thorough audits based on the training I have received.

My Canadian regulator observed me for two days. Throughout the observation period, he did not let on if I was doing things right or wrong. It was my responsibility to conduct my audit as if he wasn't there. It was a true audit, not a test. So, I tried to do my best work, the way I always do.

At the conclusion of the second day, he sat me down and gave me feedback.

"What I have noticed is that your audit time is not proportional in relation to your procedure review and your records review," he told me. "You spend a disproportionate amount of time on procedure."

I just looked at him. He paused, giving me the space to interject or reject his claims. I had plenty I wanted to say, but I told myself to remain quiet until the end of the feedback session.

"You spend a lot of time explaining to the client what the nonconformance issues are. Your summary should suffice," he continued.

Again, I sat silently. I gave him a nod to acknowledge that I was listening. I knew he expected me to interject, offer excuses, explain myself, or reject his feedback entirely. He was accustomed to such reactions. I knew better. I had my reasons I do things the way I do, but it wasn't time to discuss my side yet.

He shared a few more items and then stopped.

"Mr. Raza, don't you have anything you want to say or add?" he asked, almost in disbelief.

"I was waiting until you had concluded giving feedback," I replied. "I have no reason to interrupt you."

He did not respond, but his eyebrows, a tell-tale body-language sign, showed a surprise.

If I had interrupted him while he was giving me feedback, he would not have been in "feedback receiving mode." He was so focused on delivering his side of the audit that interrupting him would have been met with unfavorable results.

By allowing him to speak before I interjected, I primed him to enter "feedback-receiving mode." He asked for feedback on his feedback! The dynamics became favorable for me to respond. I gave my response to his observations, and he understood my perspective.

I told him the reason I spent more time reviewing procedures was because there were very little records available. That is why I raised a major nonconformance. Since he was now in receiving mode, he understood the perspective and agreed with my response.

Our brains process tons of information each day. Our hearts feel so many different emotions throughout the day. We have many different interactions with advice-givers and receivers each day. Practice these tips with your friends and family.

Try to avoid "unsolicited" advice. That advice comes from generalizations and advice on personality and attitudes. A tangible situation calls for tangible advice. Be direct. Be genuine. Be open to possibility.

Summary:

- *Advice is structured information that one person offers to another, to impact a choice or behavior.*

- *When giving advice, make the receiver feel safe, offer advice on specific and observable behaviors. Don't advise on personal characteristics or attitude and describe the observable behavior.*

- *When receiving advice, be receptive, avoid getting defensive, listen with your heart. Don't respond immediately, have a conversation, and appreciate the feedback no matter what.*

Chapter 17: Moving Forward with Awareness

From Myers-Briggs to ego, to passive-aggressiveness, to the art of giving advice, with many important topics in between. I hope you have enjoyed this journey with me. I enjoyed sharing my stories and teachable moments with you.

As you look at your life and make steps to these topics to your professional and personal endeavors, I have a few parting inspirations.

Change Takes Time

Imagine you are starting a new diet and trying to lose weight. After one week of eating healthy, you don't see any weight loss results. By week two, you see results, but they are quite small. You begin to get discouraged. You thought this diet would lead you to complete your goals! Well, it probably will, but it takes time and patience.

The same can be said for applying the principles in this book. It takes time to figure out what exactly triggers your ego. It takes time to realize what your triggers are and how to control them in moments of conflict.

It takes time to apply a universal blanket of awareness over everything you see, do, and encounter. It takes time to change old habits and ways of thinking.

I'm still working on many of the elements in this book. It is a lifelong journey marked with increments of breakthroughs and "aha" moments. Cherish those moments and don't give up.

You will get out of the box. You will find the strength to confront your passive-aggressive boss. You will apply a new level of understanding to those around you because you see everyone has something of value to offer. It just won't happen all at once. We just need to continually apply the lessons throughout our lives.

When you start eating healthy vegetables, your body may fight back. It craves the processed food and sugar it was accustomed to. The same can be said for your mind as you embark on this awareness journey. Your ego, your mind, and your preconceived notions of how the world works will fight back and provide resistance to the positive change you are making. Remember: this is a test. You can overcome it!

Never Stop Learning

While we've covered a lot of ground throughout this book, my suggestions and examples are just very small slivers in a much greater pie. Never stop learning! Go out and read about different personality type indicator tests. Dive into a deeper level of ego by exploring some Sigmund Freud. Research these topics on the internet.

Have meaningful conversations about them over coffee with friends. I hope this book has ignited a spark within you to never stop learning and never stop exploring. I hope this is a good foundation for you to become an emotionally intelligent adventurer into the many tools, theories, talks, and experiences that exist in our world.

Follow Through

It is one thing to read a book and think, "Well, that was interesting." It is another thing to read a book and apply the lessons and theories within it to your own life. I hope you try! I hope you determine your personality indicator type. I hope you have fun discovering the personality indicators of those closest to you. I hope you can identify the times in your life when you've been a sheep, donkey, fox, or owl. I hope you learn to identify the intensity of your feelings and your goals for how you want to feel in a particular moment.

Stay Connected

As a lifelong learner, I have created a space for us to share stories, learn from one another, and support each other based on what we've experienced together in this book. I invite you to share your stories with us on the blog at SalmanRaza.net or TheLifeNC.com.

When my wife left the workforce after giving birth to our son, she was craving a social outlet. We lived in a small village in England, and she was used to working and being around people. That was around the time she stumbled upon the National Childcare Trust.

My wife joined a group of women who were also mothers, both new and seasoned; a group of women going through the same thing at the same time. They discussed babies who were not sleeping, and teething, tummy bugs, vaccinations, and more. The babies in the group were growing at the same time, around the same ages.

The mothers felt comfortable in their social circle of like minds and similar experiences. My wife had an outlet for feedback and advice as she navigated motherhood for the first time. It was such a relatable network. It was a huge gift to us. If she had a question, she could ask her group and receive validation on her gut instinct or advice on a new approach.

That is what this group is all about. We might not navigate the waters of motherhood together, but we can journey together on a path of awareness, tranquility, balance, empathy, and wisdom. I hope to learn from you. By sharing our unique perspectives, we can create a beautiful culture and community of learning and growing.

If you have read this book and benefitted from the theories I have shared, we can become a community where we share our experiences fearlessly, without feeling defensive, without fear of being judged.

Vulnerability opens us up. It allows us to be open to things such as teachable moments, self-awareness, and awareness of others. Vulnerability gives us the opportunity to be perfectly flawed and human. Vulnerability may just be one of the special things that can calm down a triggered ego.

Let's be vulnerable together.

Summary:

- *Change takes time; it is a constant evolution.*
- *Never stop learning; seek out more information on the topics that interest you.*
- *Stay connected; we learn from one another in community.*

THE END